Ahmed Ginaidi

JESUS CHRIST AND MARY FROM QUR'ANIC-ISLAMIC PERSPECTIVE

Fundamental Principles for Dialogue between Islam and Christianity

Translated from the German

by Christa Ginaidi

Ahmed Ginaidi

JESUS CHRIST AND MARY FROM QUR'ANIC-ISLAMIC PERSPECTIVE

Fundamental Principles for Dialogue between Islam and Christianity

Edition Noema
Stuttgart

Bibliografische Information Der Deutschen Bibliothek

Die Deutsche Bibliothek verzeichnet diese Publikation in der Deutschen Nationalbibliografie; detaillierte bibliografische Daten sind im Internet über <http://dnb.ddb.de>rufbar.

∞

Gedruckt auf alterungsbeständigem, säurefreien Papier
Printed on acid-free paper

ISBN: 3-89821-585-7

© *ibidem*-Verlag

Stuttgart 2005
Alle Rechte vorbehalten

Das Werk einschließlich aller seiner Teile ist urheberrechtlich geschützt. Jede Verwertung außerhalb der engen Grenzen des Urheberrechtsgesetzes ist ohne Zustimmung des Verlages unzulässig und strafbar. Dies gilt insbesondere für Vervielfältigungen, Übersetzungen, Mikroverfilmungen und elektronische Speicherformen sowie die Einspeicherung und Verarbeitung in elektronischen Systemen.

Printed in Germany

To my wife Christa

FOREWORD 9

1. The Principle of the Relationship to God – Man Within Islamic Dogmatics... 15
1.1 Who is this Allah for the Muslims? 17
1.2 The Interaction of Man as Creature before God the Creator.. 25
1.3 The Human Being as Creature of God and God's Mercy to Him.. 31
1.4 The Perspective according to Islamic Theology 35
1.5 The Function of the Bi-polarity in Humanity 41
1.6 Islam and Original Sin 48
1.7 The Price for Khalifate of Humanity 53
1.8 Satan as Personification of Human Inadequacy 63
1.9 The Islamic Path to God 69

2. The Origin of Mary, the Mother of Jesus 83
2.1 The Problem in the Ancestry of Mary 85
2.2 The Testimony in the Qur'an about the Position of Mary 89
2.3 The Portrayal of Mary from Islamic Sunnah 93

3. Assertions about Jesus from the Qur'an 101
3.1 The Prophecy of Jesus.. 101
3.2 The Birth of Jesus 114
3.3   Life and Work of Jesus from the Point of View in the Qur'an 128
3.4 The " Passing" of Jesus 151

4. Common Statements about Jesus and Mary in the Qur'an and the Bible as an Elementary Basis for Dialogue between the Religions 167

7

5. Different Statements about Mary and Jesus in the Holy Scriptures 181

6. Possibilities of a Mutual Understanding as a Basis for Communication 203

BIBLIOGRAPHY 211

FOREWORD

The reason for writing this book comes out of my religious experience in the diaspora, the Muslim people scattered in non-Muslim cultures. In the early sixties as I was completing my practical education in mechanical engineering in Germany, I had to decline the free milk, which was provided by the company for the workers. I did this because of religious dietary restrictions in spite of the strenuous work welding. My religious piety aroused reactions of my coworkers. This ranged from railing against the medieval practice of fasting to discussions about its meaning including my ability to keep working hard while fasting. This Islamic practice of fasting has made me able to conquer my weaker self. Thanks to this I am not addicted to anything or dependant on any substance to live my life.

Another experience which prompted me to write this book is the condition of the Muslims in the diaspora. First, many Muslims are not aware of the importance of Jesus and his mother Mary according to Islamic doctrine. Secondly, I had an experience at the beginning of my teaching career that increased my interest in theology. One day I met a Turkish pupil outside his classroom. This was incomprehensible to me. When I asked the student why he was not in class, he explained to me that he had a free period because his classmates had religious education. They are Christians whereas he is Muslim.

This explanation made me reflect because in his situation I would have acted just like him. So I became aware of an exclusionary policy that unavoidably leads to an alienation of Muslim pupils both among classmates at school and within the Christian society in which they live. These experiences combined with my knowledge from more than 30 years in the field of Christian-Islamic dialogue, life in Germany and the cultural problems inside a modern society showed and proved to me the challenge. The so-called modern man has more than he really needs materially. However, the inherent necessity to believe is nipped in the bud by the predominant majority of the population. The results of this cannot be ignored.

The possibility of an individual's union with God's Creation and feeling a sense of becoming one with it will not be attained through a lack of religion or spirituality. The consequence is personal dissatisfaction which affects interaction with others resulting in higher rates of alcoholism, drug addiction, depression, divorce rates, suicide, etc.

The intention of this book is to show the Christian reader a new perspective from the essence of one's own faith in the hope of confirming it. There are other books presently addressing this topic. These books treat the differences in the doctrine relating to Jesus from the Islamic and Christian viewpoints by brushing them under the proverbial rug. Such a procedure is dishonest to both Messages from God because these differences constitute precisely the richness in God's offer to mankind.

The Islam is the only post Christian religion descendant from Abraham, which confirms Jesus as a legitimate emissary of God. The fact that there is not absolute similarity creates a more lively dialogue. I am very concerned about the honesty in the description of Christ from the Islamic viewpoint and precisely where there is not absolute similarity. I assume that with the help of God we will be able to communicate with each other never the less positively.

I feel committed to the Western civilization because its people have accepted my intellectual achievements and therefore I want to have a personal share in fostering peace in this culture. This culture's wealth is due in large parts to its diversity.

In this regard I cannot forget my German wife, who was formerly Roman Catholic. She converted to Islam against my will. This book would not have been feasible without her and her support in every aspect, as well as her capability to type with 10 fingers. Of primary importance was the correct theological consciousness of my own religion. This was first necessary in contrast to Christianity to show me the wisdom of God revealing himself by Judaism, Christianity and Islam. I would like to give the Christian reader of this book this experience to accompany him on his journey through life.

The content of this book has been written to the best of my knowledge and belief in the conscious awareness of the full responsibility before God. Therefore I endeavoured to represent the commentary of the Qur'an according to the official opinion of Islam and its highest authority of the Al-Azhar-University in Cairo. Quotations from this commentary are marked accordingly. This edition has been authorized by the signature of the dean of the faculty for the Fundamental Principles of Islam, Professor Doctor Mahmoud Hamdi Zakzuk on 10/10/1995.

This book affects all of Christianity in the world. Therefore, it is extremely important for me and my wife to make it available to many people. My wife, who is an English teacher, agreed to translate this book from German into English. All quotations are translated into English and afterwards the original text is quoted in square brackets. In the verses of the Qur'an and since ch. 1.2 the term "Allah" is translated by "God".

My wife and I would like to thank one of our best friends, our brother Reverend John-Paul Meyer in Rocklin, California, with all our hearts for his linguistic support.

1. The Principle of the Relationship to God – Man Within Islamic Dogmatics

Before I go into the actual subject I want to discuss in this chapter the fundamental principles of the relationship between man and God in Islam. Let us begin with the Arabic term "Allah" for God. Since Jews and Christians living in Islamic countries apply the same term as the Arabian concept for God, it is important to mention the origin of this word "Allah".

The term "ilah" was the common expression for a god. The fact that you find here the phonetic similarity with the Hebrew word "eloah" points to a common Semitic root. From linking the term "Allah" with the Arabic definite article "al", i.e. "the" merges with the article to form "al-ilah", "the God" (cp. Schwarzenau 1977, 102). "In other words, it was common practice to speak about 'god' in general terms, for example, about Hubal or another specifically limited single god. That does not mean that already in Pre-Islamic Arabia the many individual gods would have been merged in the one and exclusive God. Monotheism was still by no means accepted" (ibid. 102). ["Mit anderen Worten, es war gang und gäbe, von 'Gott' überhaupt zu sprechen, anstatt etwa von Hubal oder irgendeinem anderen mehr oder weniger begrenzten Einzelgott. Damit ist allerdings noch nicht gesagt, dass schon im vorislamischen Arabien die vielen Einzelgötter in den einen und alleinigen Gott aufgegangen wären. Der Monotheismus hatte sich noch keineswegs durchgesetzt"].

Up to the time of Islam the term „ Allah " had no connection to the concept of monotheism. Over time the differentiation occurred through revelation in the Qur'an between Allah whom the Prophet taught and allah whom the Arabs recognized up to that time. In surah 39, 36 you can find such a reference: "Is not God enough for His servant? But they try to frighten thee with other (gods) besides Him! for such as God leaves to stray, there can be no guide." (Surah is the equivalent to a chapter. So surah 39, 38 is chapter 39, verse 36.)

Here you can clearly see the difference between the many gods who also had the name "allah" and "Allah" whom the Prophet uniquely introduced. The difference between Allah of the Prophet and the other allah is cited in surah 29, 61: "If indeed thou ask them who has created the heavens and the earth and subjected the sun and the moon (to His Law), they will certainly reply, "God." How are they then deluded away (from the truth)?"

According to similar verses which you can abundantly find in the Qur'an, the content of the Arabic article "al" which is equivalent to "the" means "unique". Exactly this change of meaning marks the birth of the monotheistic concept (cp. Ginaidi 2002, 204).

1.1 Who is this Allah for the Muslims?

In Islam God constitutes the centre of faith. Who is then this God (Allah)? In order to speak about the attributes of God I cannot overlook the first surah of the Qur'an, "The Opening":

"1 In the name of God, Most Gracious, Most Merciful. 2 Praise be to God, the Cherisher and Sustainer of the worlds; 3 Most Gracious, Most Merciful; 4 Master of the Day of Judgment. 5 Thee do we worship, and Thine aid we seek, 6 Show us the straight way, 7 The way of those on whom Thou hast bestowed Thy Grace, those whose (portion) is not wrath, and who go not astray." Here the Prophet speaks "In the name of God, the most Gracious, the most Merciful", by which almost every chapter in the Qur'an begins. For mankind God is a merciful and gracious God. That fits very well with the human insufficiency and gives an opportunity to every "sinner" to better himself. In this the intelligent human being recognizes that God knows very well about the attributes of the creature created by Him whose name is man. It is comforting for every human being to know that this merciful God will reign on the day of the Last Judgement, in other words, everybody can depend on God's mercy. The verses 6 and 7 of this surah contain a human petition to Him and everybody may hope to be guided by God.

How am I as a human being supposed to think of God? Surah 112 contains concrete references to Him: "In the name of God, Most Gracious, Most Merciful. 1 Say: He is God, the

One and Only; 2 God, the Eternal, Absolute; 3 He begetteth not, nor is He begotten; 4 And there is none like unto Him."

The whole Qur'an references a part of the Divine attributes. His nature is incomprehensible for us as human beings. "God is the highest cosmic magnitude, but also an ideal which cannot be comprehended by any philosophic speculation. Unique in His nature G. determines the path of events in the world. In His omnipotence life and power are united. His wisdom means the knowledge of the future. Here is the origin of the Islamic teachings of the predestination" (Khoury 1987, 426). ["God ist die höchste kosmische Größe, aber auch ein Ideal, das von keinerlei philosophischer Spekulation erfasst werden kann. Einmalig in seinem Wesen, bestimmt G. den Lauf der Dinge in der Welt. In seiner Allmacht sind Leben und Kraft vereinigt. Seine Weisheit bedeutet die Kenntnis des Kommenden. Hier liegt der Ursprung der islamischen Lehre von der Vorherbestimmung"]. The part of the quotation „ G. determines the path of events in the world" refers to Divine providence and this is the basis for a fatalistic attitude for many muslims. I will go into this special problem later. On this point Abu Zahra (he died in 1974) mentions that God gives each creature the power to definitely act, but what he does comes through the permission of God and is subjected to the power of God (cp. ibid. 426).

This belongs to God's attributes as the superior Creator, the sovereign ruler and judge of His creatures (cp. Kreiser 1974 vol. 1, 36). The words from the throne in surah 2, 255, further clarify the attributes of God: "God! There is no god but He, the Living, the Self-subsisting, Eternal. No slumber can seize Him nor sleep. His are all things in the heavens and on earth. Who is there can intercede in His presence except as He permitteth? He knoweth what (appeareth to His creatures as) Before or After or Behind them. Nor shall they compass aught of His knowledge except as He willeth. His Throne doth extend over the heavens and the earth, and He feeleth no fatigue in guarding and preserving them for He is the Most High, the Supreme (in glory)."

In the above-mentioned verse the might of God is defined clearly and precisely. That God with His concentrated power is nearer to man than his jugular vein is shown in verse 16 in surah 50: "It was We Who created man, and We know what dark suggestions his soul makes to him: for We are nearer to him than (his) jugular vein."

The Arabian name for God "Allah" theologically expresses the uniqueness of God. This name differentiates itself from the ancient gods before Islam. God is unique and singularly one. "The most fundamental and most important part of the teachings of the Prophet Mohammed is the belief in the unity of God. This is expressed in the first Kalima, the fundamental creed of Islam which is in Arabic 'la ilaha illa-llah' - 'there is no deity except God'. This wonderful statement is the basis of Islam, its foundation and its most essential part" (Maudoodi 1978, 90). ["Der grundsätzlichste und wichtigste Bestandteil der Lehre des Propheten Muhammad ist der Glaube an die Einheit Gottes. Dies wird ausgedrückt in der ersten Kalima, dem fundamentalen Glaubensbekenntnis des Islams, das auf arabisch lautet: 'la illaha illa-llah' - ‚es gibt keine Gottheit außer Gott'. Dieser wunderschöne Satz ist die Grundlage des Islams, sein Fundament und sein wesentlichster Bestandteil."]

About the concept „ Allah " Paul Schwarzenau writes: „God is the word as it is expressed in the prologue of the Gospel of John which refers to the Counselor. Allah is God and Allah is also His name.

Originally the English word "God", in German "Gott" was a neuter noun, guddam, which means simply 'The Proclaimed One'. The Teutons understood Christ as God being the same as 'The Proclaimed One': the God who rules over the history of the world.

Islam expresses this in its symbol, the creed, branding in a script of flame in Arabic characters that emphasizes the circle surrounding them as a sign of unity – the blazing name of Allah" (Schwarzenau 1977, 139 et seq.). ["Gott ist das Wort, wie das auf den Parakleten verweisende Johannesevangelium in seinem Prolog sagt. Gott ist nicht Begriff, sondern Wort oder Name. God ist Gott und der Name in einem.

Das deutsche Wort Gott war ursprünglich ein Neutrum, guddam, das soviel wie das ‚Ausgerufene' bedeutete. Unter dem Eindruck des Gottes Christi verstanden die Germanen, dass dieser Gott nur der Eine Ausgerufene sein konnte: das Ausgerufensein Gottes, das eine ganze Weltzeit überruft.

Der Islam bringt das in seinem Symbol, dem zur Flammenschrift arabischer Schriftzeichen auflohenden Glaubensbekenntnis, das den diese als Ganzheitszeichen umschließenden Kreis noch überloht, als Flammenschrift Allahs zum Ausdruck"].

So Schwarzenau expresses the significance of giving this name. What is important is not an expression for God but proclaiming one of His most important characteristics, namely His absolute uniqueness. Statements about the attributes of God are based on the understanding of His uniqueness. The theological content of His attributes as the only one are expressed already in giving the name of God, i.e. "Allah".

With this it should be pointed out that God is not out of reach for men, but that He determines solely how near or far away He is for us. His mercy, however, is one of the most generous gifts to every individual. This uniqueness of God presented a revolution in the religious experience of the Arabs at that time.

As in the time before Islam the relationship between the members of a clan provided a tie for survival and continuity within a clan, so all the deities before Islam were sons and daughters of one god. At that time it was not possible for men to imagine God as a being without relationship. Precisely here surah 112, which at that time was a completely new revelation, makes the point. The existence of a Divine being without forefathers and without a "clan" nevertheless has immense power initiated rethinking in regards to theology.

The Qur'an has many verses pertaining to God, His omnipotence, His knowledge and many other of His attributes. In the following chapter the relationship between God and human beings shall be considered, mainly in order to point out the foundation of Islamic theology and the action of God inside the way of human life in general as well as the particular articulation of the Islamic behaviour as it pertains to the situation in the diaspora.

1.2 The Interaction of Man as Creature before God the Creator

The foundation for interaction between man and God is the basic Islamic understanding of God. The following verse, 2, 117, demonstrates that He is the Creator of everything: "To Him is due the primal origin of the heavens and the earth: when He decreeth a matter, He saith to it: "Be," and it is." This imperative "Be!" refers both to dead and living matter known to man as well as the things of which men have had no knowledge until now. The conclusion of surah 23, 12-14 is that humanity is a product of God's Creation: "12 Man We did create from a quintessence (of clay); 13 Then We placed him as (a drop of) sperm in a place of rest, firmly fixed; 14 Then We made the sperm into a clot of congealed blood; then of that clot We made a (foetus) lump; then We made out of that lump bones and clothed the bones with flesh; then We developed out of it another creature. So blessed be God, the Best to create!" These verses make clear the basic understanding of man as God's creature together with all the other creatures He made. It must be stated here that the two terms "heaven" and "earth" are used totally differently than the understanding in the ancient church. According to the Qur'an there is not just one heaven and one earth but many of them. As a result earth is not a disc with the heaven put over it but comparing the earth with an egg is revealed in the Qur'an. Now back to the actual content of this chapter:

A similarity of God with man analogous to the Christian portrayal of man in the image of God doesn't exist in the Qur'an. Man is a creature of God. This self-image of man ought to influence his relation to the other creatures of God in a positive way, in other words: respect for other beings should be self-evident! To what extent this Islamic emphasis is taken into account in everyday life is an absolutely different question of course.

Therefore as a creature, man isn't different from the other beings. With this awareness every Muslim can take comfort facing life's difficulties, because there is comfort in this combined with the mercy of God. It provides a dependable barrier and protection from every form of overestimation of human ability and pride.

The basis for the relationship to God the Almighty is expressed in surah 6, 103: "No vision can grasp Him. But His grasp is over all vision: He is above all comprehension, yet is acquainted with all things." This way God the Almighty already knows the needs of men before they actually are aware of them. If something negative is happening to a person and he can't do anything about this, his faith is challenged to accept this as given by God. Exactly here is the essence of the term "Islam", that is to be Muslim.

Thus, the genus of the human race as a created entity is absolutely dependent on its Creator. The freedom of people in which they can live out their creative abilities has been granted to them by God. A happy person is the one who is conscious of this gift of God and who accepts these concrete gifts – this means all the human capabilities with whose help a man can form his own life within this freedom permitted by God and he shapes his life accordingly. "So the commitment to the own nature as creature necessitates a radical reversal of thinking which also alters the behaviour of the believer: Presumption, pride in possessions, boasting about the number and powerful relatives, everything issued from missing the insight into mankind's nature as a creature is recognized as reprehensible; covetousness, deceit in weights and measures, embezzlement of property, abuse of weaker persons, resorting to violence, all this has to cease so that at God who meticulously keeps an account of everything, may reckon the foul deeds do not exceed the good deeds" (Nagel 1994, 27 et seq.). ["So macht das Bekenntnis zur eigenen Kreatürlichkeit eine tiefgreifende Umkehr des Denkens notwendig, die auch das Handeln des Gläubigen umgestaltet: Anmaßung, Stolz auf den Besitz, Prahlen mit einer zahlreichen und mächtigen Verwandtschaft, alles floß aus der fehlenden Einsicht in die Kreatürlichkeit und wird jetzt als verwerflich erkannt; Raffgier, Betrug beim Messen und Wiegen, Veruntreuung fremden Eigentums, grobe Beschimpfung Schwächerer, Anwendung von Gewalt, das alles muß unterbleiben, damit bei Allah, der peinlich genau über alles Buch führt, das Konto der bösen Taten nicht das der guten überwiege."]

This is stated in surah 2, 281: "And fear the Day when ye shall be brought back to God. Then shall every soul be paid what it earned, and none shall be dealt with unjustly." This verse also defines the limits of human freedom, which has just been mentioned. The affirmation of one's own nature as a creature inside Islamic theology largely anticipates the acting of God in His capacity as Most Gracious, Most Merciful. However God is not a sadist who equips man with negative attributes in order to punish him afterwards. Thus 2, 286 says: "On no soul doth God place a burden greater than it can bear. It gets every good that it earns, and it suffers every ill that it earns. (Pray:) "Our Lord! Condemn us not if we forget or fall into error; our Lord! Lay not on us a burden like that which Thou didst lay on those before us; our Lord! lay not on us a burden greater than we have strength to bear. Blot out our sins, and grant us forgiveness. Have mercy on us. Thou art our Protector; help us against those who stand against Faith." This verse describes exactly how a weak soul who has slipped up has to behave with regard to God. The most important point is that God doesn't place a burden on anyone greater than he can accomplish. God most definitely accepts everybody in spite of trespasses. Yet every individual has to take into consideration that the last decision (judgement) is left to God. Therefore, everyone who is only trying a little bit to do the good in line along with his weakness may trust that this benefits him. There is a further confirmation of these facts of the case in 2, 233: "…No soul shall have a burden laid on it greater than it can bear."

What seems contradictory to the reader of the Islamic Holy Scripture is on closer inspection nothing else than a demonstration of opposing perspectives in order to point out the contrast. Historic examples or apparent contradictory passages are in reality nothing other than limitations, which define the freedom of humanity as a created entity. "The picture of humanity in the Qur'an shifts between two poles; one the one hand human beings are in the position of slaves before God as Lord of the Creation, on the other hand they are the representatives of God in the world, too" (Bürgel 1991, 35). ["Das koranische Menschenbild bewegt sich zwischen zwei Polen; denn einerseits befindet sich der Mensch in einer Sklavenstellung gegenüber Gott als dem Herrn der Schöpfung; zum anderen ist er aber auch Stellvertreter Gottes auf Erden."]

Every individual has to decide which position he wants to take within the freedom granted by the Creator while respecting the limits of this freedom. God's power is demonstrated clearly in the aforementioned verse. That this God with His unbridled power is nearer to a human being than his jugular vein is shown in verse 16 in surah 50: "It was We Who created man, and We know what dark suggestions his soul makes to him: for We are nearer to him than (his) jugular vein."

1.3 The Human Being as Creature of God and God's Mercy to Him

Considering the powers placed at the disposal of humanity which control the human being within his freedom on earth the following principles must be pointed out:

- Fundamentally the conscience of people which controls behaviour is valid.

- Human reason is given to humanity as a gift of God to accompany them on the path of life.

- Human feelings are entrusted to humanity by God as an important distinguishing feature from the angels.

- There is a tension between the human reason and the inherent feelings and inclination of mankind.

In an Islamic environment a person is led as a result of following the ritual prayer, fasting and socializing with others to a religion in which he is integrally and completely oriented to God. This conscious orientation to God results in correct behaviour. Through upbringing this process either will be strengthened or killed. Within the passages of maturation God is acting as an internal psychological power influencing people's behaviour. From this the human being gains his self-awareness and the mental energy for his actions. The kindness of God toward humanity is described in surah 2, verse 30: "Behold, thy Lord said to the angels: "I will create a vicegerent on earth." They said: "Wilt Thou place therein one who will make mischief therein and shed blood? Whilst we do celebrate Thy praise and glorify Thy holy (name)?" He said: "I know what ye know not."

The idea of the human being as representative of God holds an enormous danger. That could open the floodgates of human pride. Men could understand themselves as "representatives of God" on earth.

Here it is important to include the parallel to Christianity in the discussion. The term "incarnation of Jesus" implies the fact that man is similar to God, because Jesus has been one of them and at the same time personifies God incarnate. That is a fatal mistake of the Christian who is theologically ignorant. According to the Christian theology the similarity of man to God means nothing else than the amount of reason God has given to Adam to take with him on his journey through life.

This equates with the Islamic understanding of man's relationship to God.

The Christian misunderstanding of the nature of mankind naturally has frightful consequences concerning the Christian relating to his fellow man as well as to the environment. This position is the opposite of the life of Jesus, for according to Islam Jesus' behaviour represents the crown of humility.

This above-mentioned misconception of many Christians is the absolute contradiction of the Islamic spirit of devotion under the will of God. Under this misconception humanity would be anything other than a Creation of God. The term "representative" as a designation for man in dialogue with the angels immediately before the Creation of Adam, as expressed in the above quoted verse, constitutes God's highest gift to humanity. In order to understand this verse correctly you have to understand the thought pattern of the people who have received the Islamic Message. At that time and up to this day it isn't allowed to accept any offered gift, no matter where it comes from, as it is given. In the severe desert life of the Bedouins this custom was established. The Bedouins speak to each other with very gracious, noble expressions. However, materially they must be extremely frugal. The supplier offers a good deal more than he wants to give actually. Taking these facts into account and applying them to the relationship to God – the individual has a good deal more of it if he doesn't regard himself as the representative of God but knowing that he is important to God is more than he is allowed to hope for.

1.4 The Perspective according to Islamic Theology

The perspective according to Islamic theology in the official explanation of the Qur'an of this verse is interesting. It is done by the Muslim World League in Mecca and authenticated by the dean of the faculty for fundamentals of Islam from the Al-Azhar-University in Cairo. "It seems that the angels, though they are holy and pure and equipped by

God with particular abilities, represent only one part of the Creation. We have to imagine them probably without passions and movements of the soul whose noblest blossom is love. If emotions were given to man so these emotions could carry him in the heights or throw him into the depths. The ability of free decision, to choose by his own had to come along with these emotions so that man may navigate the ship of his life. The capability to decide with free will (provided that he used it correctly) gave mankind a certain amount of control over his own fate and over nature. Thereby he was brought closer to the Divine Being who has the highest power. We can assume that angels don't have an independent will of their own. Their perfection in other fields reflects the perfection of God. However it couldn't raise them to the high rank of God's sovereignty. The perfect governor or representative has the capability and the right to act on his own initiative, yet his independent actions always reflect exactly the will of his master. Angels due to their one-sidedness only saw the disaster which results from the abuse of nature by man when dominated by emotion; Maybe because they were without emotion, they didn't understand the total nature of God who gives and demands love. In humility and devotion to God they object" (Die Bedeutung des Korans 1996, 28 et seq.).

["Es scheint, daß die Engel, obwohl sie heilig und rein und von Gott mit bestimmten Fähigkeiten ausgestattet sind, nur eine Seite der Schöpfung darstellen. Wir müssen sie uns wohl ohne Leidenschaften und Gemütsbewegungen vorstellen, deren edelste Blüte die Liebe ist. Wenn der Mensch mit Gefühlen begabt werden sollte, so konnte ihn diese Gefühle in höchster Höhe tragen oder in tiefste Tiefe stürzen. Die Fähigkeit, sich frei zu entscheiden, selbst zu wählen, musste mit diesen Gefühlen einhergehen, damit der Mensch das Steuer seines Lebensschiffs selbst in der Hand habe. Die Fähigkeit der freien Willensentscheidung verlieh ihm (sofern er sie richtig nutzte) in gewissem Umfang die Herrschaft über sein eigenes Geschick und über die Natur. Dadurch wurde er dem Göttlichen Wesen nähergebracht, das die höchste Gewalt und den absoluten Willen besitzt. Wir können annehmen, dass die Engel keinen eigenen, unabhängigen Willen besitzen. Ihre Vollkommenheit auf anderen Gebieten spiegelt die Vollkommenheit Gottes wider. Doch vermochte sie nicht, sie in den hohen Rang der Statthalterschaft Gottes zu erheben. Der vollkommene Statthalter oder Stellvertreter ist der, der die Fähigkeit und das Recht des eigenen Handelns hat, dessen selbständiges Tun jedoch stets genau den Willen seines Herrn wiedergibt. Die Engel sahen infolge ihrer Einseitigkeit nur das Unheil, das sich aus dem Missbrauch der von Gefühlen beherrschten Natur des Menschen ergeben kann; vielleicht verstanden sie auch, da sie selbst ohne

Gefühle waren, das Wesen Gottes in seiner Gesamtheit nicht, das Liebe gibt und fordert. In Demut und Ergebenheit in Gott machen sie ihre Bedenken geltend."]

Hence you can conclude the following: God is the Creator of everything, both angels and human beings. Angels are equipped with only good attributes and obey Him blindly. Mankind is provided with emotion and affections causing ambivalent situations in which he has to choose with the help of reason his behaviour between obedience and disobedience according to God's decrees. Here is the difference of mankind from the angels according to the current official Islamic theology i.e. these are the qualities which turn the human being into the "representative" of God according to the spirit of the Islam.

Just the consciousness of being designated as God's "representative" implies knowing a dependence on God and on His guidance according to His commandments and bans (cp. Ginaidi 2002, 210 et seq.).

Humans, who transgress the requirements of God, have a low threshold, which they cross with their negative behaviour. They belong to those according to Islam who are commended to God's mercy. „The unbelievers, the polytheists, stand outside of this relationship with God. They actually are not considered as humans or as only crippled spiritual souls: 'In their hearts is an illness' and they are 'deaf, mute and blind'. The Qur'an refers to these physical defects several times and in addition also emphasizes their incurableness " (Bürgel 1991, 35). ["Die Ungläubigen dagegen, die Polytheisten, stehen außerhalb dieser Beziehung zu Gott, sie werden eigentlich gar nicht als Menschen oder jedenfalls nur als geistig-seelische Krüppel gewertet: ‚In ihren Herzen ist eine Krankheit' und sie sind ‚taub, stumm und blind'. Auf diese Gebrechen weist der Koran mehrfach hin und betont zudem auch ihre Unheilbarkeit."] Their last judgement of course is a matter left to God. Why there are such men can only be a matter of speculation within the framework of Islamic theology. Such speculation is to be performed with extreme moral caution, as it seems to be an improper evaluation of God's acting and judging. One has to accept God's decision as a lesson for a person endeavouring for the good things. Here first of all the motto is valid: "His will be done" without ifs and buts.

An analogy to this behaviour is in the following very apparent example: A king's son who mingles with the crowd has to justify his behaviour to the king respective to his origin. If he behaves miserably he has to make sure that the king's reputation will not be damaged. That's how humanity must view its behaviour before the goodness of God, who also is the final judge.

This calls to mind the character of Jesus. For Muslims Jesus is anything but a son of God, because God has neither sons nor daughters and humanity according to Islam is only one of His creatures. Historically Jesus is one of the best examples how one must follow God's call. It is apparent that God equipped him with many abilities, for example to cure sick people or even to raise them from the dead. Nevertheless he behaved in a God-fearing manner and stayed within the limits predetermined by God. From this perspective he is an outstanding example not only for Christians but for all humanity in his attitude and way of life toward God and fellow men. This character all those sent by God have shown us.

1.5 The Function of the Bi-polarity in Humanity

As protection against arrogance and in order to emphasize God's omnipotence the Qur'an demonstrates to humanity the deepest root of their origin in surah 15, 26 et sqq.: "26 We created man from sounding clay, from mud moulded into shape; 27 And the Jinn race, We had created before, from the fire of a scorching wind. 28 Behold! thy Lord said to the angels: "I am about to create man, from sounding clay, from mud moulded into shape; 29 "When I have fashioned him (in due proportion) and breathed into him of My spirit, fall ye down in obeisance unto him." Having a noble origin is extremely important not only for the Arabian people then and now, it is extremely important to all human consciousness. It is common knowledge that clay consists of soil that is dust and this exactly is a symbol for "dirt". Everybody tries to get rid of dirt in his home. This shows humanity very painfully their true origin or genesis. This origin without God's acting would not be noble to thinking people. Exactly in the narrative of Creation humanity recognizes that it doesn't have a common origin with God. Therefore mortal man may not and cannot have a common nature like God in spite of his higher position as "representative" awarded by God.

The polarity is inherent to the human genus, on the one hand he is created from "dirt", on the other hand, he becomes by God's spirit what they are now. Thanks to His grace what he is can be projected onto the life, which Jesus lived as an example before us. Because there are a lot of Muslims who think Jesus exists only for Christians and many Christians assume Jesus only belongs to them, I was motivated to write this book. That is why all the Abrahamic revelations of God are deeply related to Abraham. This diversity makes deep sense for every sensible Jew, Christian and Muslim.

In the previously mentioned quotations you find clear emphasis and demonstration of the Almighty's power. This proof of human origin is the source of humility in his secular life. The ambivalent form of revelation in the Qur'an is clearly exemplified by enhancing the status of humanity with the angels falling down awestruck in front of this creature made of clay. One the one hand man is created from soil as base, on the other hand he is the prominence of this creature as the representative of God. You can regard this as a contradiction. But you could also rightly say: It belongs to

God's pedagogy and didactic teaching humankind in tension regarding his existence.

A glance to the end of human life confirms this. Man taken from earth turns into dust again. Knowledge about the tension of "grandeur" and "misère" (B. Pascal) of the human being is one of the common grounds between the three Abrahamic religions – and so the beginning of a dialogue among them is possible.

"As creature of God humanity is created for God; if his nature is able to develop without any influence, he is good. But the human being can be seduced. God has entrusted him with a mind and with this the power over Creation, He has turned him to His representative on earth. Reason, however, is a complex, ambiguous gift of grace: By arguments men can be tempted,…" (Nagel 1994, 29). ["Als Kreatur Gottes ist der Mensch zu Gott hin geschaffen; kann sich seine Natur ohne alle Beeinflussung entfalten, ist er gut. Aber der Mensch ist verführbar. Gott hat ihm den Verstand verliehen und hiermit die Herrschaft über die Schöpfung, er hat ihn zu seinem

Stellvertreter auf der Erde gemacht. Der Verstand aber ist eine durchaus mehrdeutige Gnadengabe: Mit Argumenten kann er die Menschen verführen,..."].

However, we must not forget the conscience with which humans are acting. If they operate in the awareness as representatives of God on earth they always will take Him into consideration. In this state of mind they will behave in the right way. If they do not, they can only damage themselves by their actions. Here is truth and wisdom of the interaction between God and humanity according to Islam.

People continually miss again and again the instinctive feeling and comprehension of the problem inside the Islamic theology concerning the interaction of man and God in the above-mentioned examples from the Qur'an. From this perspective it would make more sense to write together with Muslims about these topics rather than to discuss their dogmatics separately. You see in these books that the authors got fully involved, frankly and honestly with their whole minds into the problems. But the value for Muslims as well as for non-Muslims would increase considerably, if they would have treated this matter dialogically. The discussion in the Qur'an about this interaction in principle deals not only with human as Muslim, but rather with the human genus.

Analogous to this discussion about the relation between humanity and God from the Islamic perspective, is that I as Muslim would like to know very much how this topic is treated from the Christian perspective. In discussions with many Christian theologians and non-theologians who are my friends I recognize that the ecclesiastical office plays a big part within this relationship to humanity – God. Independent from the ecclesiastical line this office cuts both ways. One the one hand there can be a favourable effect on the individual to bring in line emotions and impulses with faith, on the other hand the individual unfortunately also can be abused, as it is proved by church history. Indeed one has learned from the negative periods of history and really changed, but the credibility unfortunately has to be renewed.

It is written in the Qur'an that the insufficiency of mortals is well-known to God. In surah 17, 9 et sqq. is a God's hint for the correct use of the mind, that is to use arguments in the right way: "9 Verily this Qur-an doth guide to that which is most right (or stable), and giveth the glad tidings to the Believers who work deeds of righteousness, that they shall have a magnificent reward; 10 And to those who believe not in the Hereafter, (it announceth) that We have prepared for them a Penalty Grievous (indeed). 11 The prayer that man should make for good, he maketh for evil; for man is given to hasty (deeds)."

These verses show us that God knows everything, also about mankind's thought patterns. Logical arguments provide no hiding-place for infidel behaviour. Only God knows why a person calls to Him. "Man is ever hasty." This statement underscores human insufficiency as a character trait. No one knows this better than the Creator of mankind. To demonstrate His mercy toward His creatures and even the most intelligent among them, God shows us in surah 17, 67, how well He knows human nature: "When distress seizes you at sea, those that ye call upon - besides Himself - leave you in the lurch! But when He brings you back safe to land, ye turn away (from Him). Most ungrateful is man!"

Jesus demonstrates this to us with his own life in the garden of Gethsemane at the Mount of Olives east of Jerusalem before his arrest on the night of the Last Supper, when he said: "My Father, if it is possible, may this cup be taken from me!" Apart from the issue whether Jesus is the Son of God or not, God lets his "Messenger" get in such a situation in order to demonstrate to humanity whom they can appeal to in just such an emergency. In spite of Jesus' fantastic God given abilities to heal lepers and to raise the dead Jesus has not bothered to appeal to God in his urgent situation.

This warning is directed to those who might hit on the idea to outwit God. The above-mentioned verse 67 in surah 17 also includes a message to those who possess the highest mental capacity. They should not take advantage of their favourable situation and thereby gain privileges, for they owe this solely to their Creator.

1.6 Islam and Original Sin

An important aspect in the relationship between God and mankind – according to Islamic teaching is that humanity is free from the curse of the "original sin". This refers to the event which led to the expulsion of Adam and Eve from paradise. According to the Islamic account Eve didn't call on Adam to pick an apple from the tree of knowledge, but in fact it was Satan who encouraged both to do this.

This account is known in Islamic teaching, but it isn't an event, which overshadows the fate of all mankind. It mentions the first sin, but not, however, the original (hereditary) sin. "According to Islamic teaching there is no individual sin for which other persons could be held accountable. The fall of Mankind from Adam and Eve is only relevant in so far as it was the first of its kind. The perpetrators have repented of it; so the narrative is no more under discussion. From this perspective it is possible to understand why Islam doesn't have a baptismal ceremony of pardon from original sin. Accordingly every child is born without sin and with a natural disposition to give himself to God as Creator" (Khoury 1987, 1096 et seq.). ["Nach seiner Lehre gibt es keine Individualsünde, die in die Verantwortlichkeit anderer Menschen gelegt werden könnte. Der Sündenfall von Adam und Eva ist nur insofern theologisch relevant, als er der erste seiner Art war. Die Akteure haben ihn bereut; damit steht seine Geschichte nicht mehr zur Debatte. Diese Ausgangslage macht es begreiflich, warum der Islam die Taufe als Akt der Reinwaschung von der Erbsünde nicht kennt. Jedes Kind wird vielmehr nach seinem Konzept sündenlos und mit einer natürlichen Veranlagung, sich Gott als Schöpfer hinzugeben, geboren"]. This act of God's mercy towards the first-parents of mankind, Adam and Eve, constitutes the exact antithesis to original sin. As a result God's kindness is reborn in every newborn child. The newborn child is without sin and has the absolute freedom as a follower of God to decide in favour of good or bad.

The Islamic understanding of original sin is stated clearly in surah 7, 19-25. This also shows clearly the equality of man and woman before God: "19 O Adam! dwell thou and thy wife in the Garden, and enjoy (its good things) as ye wish: but approach not this tree, or ye run into harm and transgression." 20 Then began Satan to whisper suggestions to them, in order to reveal to them their shame that was hidden from them (before): he said: "Your Lord only forbade you this tree, lest ye should become angels or such beings as live forever." 21 And he swore to them both, that he was their sincere adviser. So by deceit he brought about their fall: when they tasted of the tree, their shame became manifest to them, and they began to sew together the leaves of the Garden over their bodies. And their Lord called unto them: "Did I not forbid you that tree, and tell you that Satan was an avowed enemy unto you?" 23 They said: "Our Lord! we have wronged our own souls: if Thou forgive us not and bestow not upon us Thy Mercy, we shall certainly be lost." 24 (God) said: "Get ye down, with enmity between yourselves. On earth will be your dwelling-place and your means of livelihood for a time." 25 He said: "Therein shall ye live, and therein shall ye die; but from it shall ye be taken out (at last)."

In this dialogue God speaks to both, Adam and Eve, as a unity. It is important, that the originator i.e. the tempter, who induced both to disobey the commandment of God, was

Satan and not Eve. Therefore, both are guilty, because they listened to Satan.

Bürgel considers that God's statement about humanity as His representative only refers to individuals. "It is correct that no case explicitly talks about ‚representative(s) of God'" (Bürgel 1991, 37). ["Richtig ist, daß in keinem Fall ausdrücklich von ‚Stellvertreter(n) Gottes' die Rede ist."] This claim cannot be accepted as stated. The counterevidence is in the following quotation from the Qur'an: "When thy Lord drew forth from the Children of Adam from their loins, their descendants, and made them testify concerning themselves, (saying): "Am I not your Lord (Who cherishes and sustains you)?" They said: "Yea! we do testify!" (this), lest ye should say on the Day of Judgment: "Of this we were never mindful." (7, 172)

The children of Adam and Adam alone form a whole not only as understood in former times, but also for our present understanding. What was valid for the father is valid also for his descendants. Here I have to repeat that the person who wants to understand other civilizations and more importantly other religions, has to first depart from his own frame of reference concerning new things or he will have great difficulty comprehending the whole field of ethnic studies. In the Qur'an Adam is the perfect example for all men – independent of affiliation to race, language and religion – as in the Bible! The responsibility of each and every one of us in dealing with the "khalifate" imposed on him by God is a proof that every human being, whether man or woman, is representative of God on earth. ("Kalif" is an understanding without exact English translation. "Successor" is the closest word. In a dynasty when the king dies his Kalif assumes the throne. God cannot die. Therefore, God cannot have a successor. "Representative" is the best English equivalent. "Disciple" or "apostle" would fit, but it could create confusion with the Christian understanding of these words.)

The expression of personal responsibility for each individual is demonstrated in surah 99, 7 et seq.: "7 Then shall anyone who has done an atom's weight of good, see it! 8 And anyone who has done an atom's weight of evil, shall see it."

Therefore the existence of priesthood i.e. monks' way of life is seen in Islam as attempt of the individuals to shirk their responsibilities imposed on them by God. "...there is no priest or monk who would be able to appropriate for himself from the treasury of grace administered by a human institution their necessary share" (Nagel 1994, 31). ["...es gibt keine Priester oder Mönche, die ihnen aus einem von einer menschlichen Institution verwalteten Gnadenschatz den notwendigen Anteil zuweisen könnten"].

1.7 The Price for Khalifate of Humanity

Human beings have been named representatives, "Khalif" of God on earth granting them freedom of choice or free will. From the Islamic viewpoint the Almighty determined their freedom wherein they are allowed to move. This chapter shall describe the conflict to which they are exposed, or in other words: How will humanity deal with God's rich blessings?

So this book does not create misunderstandings for the reader, first of all, the Islamic approach to this matter shall be differentiated from the Western Christian approach. "The question of humanity's unique position in nature still dominates modern anthropology precisely, where one distinguishes human beings from their relationship to animals; for such a study determines the conclusion concerning their distinction. The Christian-metaphysical tradition bases this unique position on the immortal spirit and soul granted only to human beings. This individual immortal soul was not simply conceived through participation in a cosmic soul, on the contrary, the biblical-Christian tradition conceives the individual soul as a celestial honour and dignity, which raises man over the whole cosmos and places him next to God in the cosmos" (Pannenberg 1983, 25). ["Die Frage nach der Sonderstellung des Menschen in der Natur beherrscht die moderne Anthropologie gerade auch da noch, wo man den Menschen aus seinem Verhältnis zum Tier begreift; denn es geht bei solcher Untersuchung ja gerade um die Feststellung des unterscheidend Menschlichen. Die christlich-metaphysische Tradition hatte diese Sonderstellung des Menschen durch den Begriff der unsterblichen Geistseele, die allein dem Menschen gegeben sei, begründet. Diese individuelle, unsterbliche Seele war nicht nur als Teilhabe an einer den Kosmos durchwaltenden Weltseele gedacht, sondern biblisch-christlich als überirdische

Auszeichnung und Würde des Menschen, die ihn über den ganzen Kosmos erhebt und ihn dem Kosmos gegenüber an die Seite Gottes stellt."] Islam can agree with this view up to a point. The two religions agree on the unique position of humanity, but there is a difference in their substance. If the uniqueness of humanity is understood as "image of God" (Gen 1, 27), doesn't it seem reasonable then to suppose that the "infinite qualitative difference" between God and human beings, between Creator and creature will become blurred? The Islamic understanding of humanity as "khalifate" opposes such blurring.

The unique position of man by no means results in an equal status of God and man. The difference guards against this and humanity remains a part of Creation. The Creator has given humanity reason. "Reason should help restrain physical urges and passions, but should not be abused with speculative understanding concerning the essence of God and Creation. For not the capability to use reason is the contrast to lack of restraint and passions, but the irrefutable knowledge of guidance going back to God" (Nagel 1994, 29). ["Der Verstand soll zur Zügelung der Triebe und Leidenschaften beitragen, nicht aber zur spekulativen Erfassung des Wesens von Gott und Schöpfung mißbraucht werden. Denn nicht das Vermögen, den Verstand zu gebrauchen, bildet den Gegensatz zu Zügellosigkeit und Leidenschaft, sondern das auf Gott selber zurückgehende Wissen von der Rechtleitung, das unwiderlegbar ist."] This brief definition of the proper use of reason is a directive for reason.

In surah 2, 31-33, is stated: "31 And He taught Adam the names of all things; then He placed them before the angels, and said: "Tell Me the names of these if ye are right." With this verse God began to prepare Adam for his position as khalif. It is important to note here that God taught Adam "the names of things". Each pedagogue knows that memory formation begins with its name. Thinking begins with the use of language.

This hint from the Qur'an states that God Himself has taught humanity reasoning and precisely this Divine attribute was withheld from angels. "32 They said: "Glory to Thee: of knowledge we have none, save what Thou hast taught us: in truth it is Thou Who art perfect in knowledge and wisdom."

This was the response of the angels to God because God taught Adam "the name of the things" and not them. "33 He said: "O Adam! Tell them their names." When he had told them, God said: "Did I not tell you that I know the secrets of heavens and earth, and I know what ye reveal and what ye conceal?" This test of Adam as representative for the humanity in contrast to the angels Adam passed with flying colours. This test was the final preparation of humanity's forefather to be God's representative on earth. With this man not only took on khalifate, but also responsibility for the vocation in the cosmos God has given him.

We should never forget this statement in the Qur'an concerning the origin of human reason. If this is the case it explains the disunity between Creation and human existence affecting all levels of the Creation, both material and spiritual. This references also the discrepancy between God's Creation and the decline of civilization with its consequences for the environment.

This God given cognitive ability for humanity's journey through life is a two-edged sword. The Qur'an gives directions to use these abilities correctly. The linguistic influence of this Holy Book on the Arabic language goes so far as to provide conversational idioms concerning behaviour.

This is illustrated by a little excursus in the Arabic language of the Qur'an. This will clarify the Islamic view dealing with reason i.e. human ability to think. A reasonable man is called in Arabic "aaqel". A human who bridles his camel is called "jaaqel" in Arabic. This "j" refers to the active form of the agent who carries out this action. So it is understood that thinking and restraining oneself have the same linguistic root. This includes careful handling of God's gift. It is not allowed to abuse God given reason. An individual should use reason correctly. This noblest possession makes us khalifs of God. It should never be used for egoistical purposes arising from personal emotion and affection.

All kinds of discord are the final result in relation to Creation and oneself when passion is not restrained i.e. the consequence of abusing reason which is a result of free will. The price humanity has to pay for this Divine gift is still with us.

"To anchor the conception of this knowledge in each believer with unsurpassable certainty is the highest aim of the Islamic theology. It is already predetermined in its revelation that this endeavour will fail without using reason granted to humanity, but before reaching the aim the demands of severe reason have to be given up" (Nagel 1994, 29). ["Dieses Wissen auf den Begriff zu bringen und in einem jeden Gläubigen mit unüberbietbarer Gewißheit zu verankern, dies ist das höchste Ziel aller islamischen Theologie, und es ist ihr schon in der Offenbarung vorgezeichnet, dass ihre Anstrengungen zwar ohne die Indienstnahme des dem Menschen geschenkten Verstandes fehlgehen müssen, dass aber stets vor dem Erreichen des Zieles unnachsichtig die Opferung der Ratio verlangt werden muß"].

However, I have to disagree with this criticism of the Islamic thought in the Qur'an. There can be no question of "giving up reason"! Rational methodology in the physical and scientific disciplines demands consideration of the natural attributes of material components and is precisely the secret of success. So it is also a precondition in order to be successful when considering the "natural" attributes of the components. But there is a rational question - who granted these "natural" attributes to matter? Is it not He who taught Adam, the first human being, the names of things? Or which reason is meant?

With the definition of "reason" you have to apply the standard of entirety. Nature as God's work is the best instructor of this. There are a few basic principles which govern macrocosm as well as microcosm. However, the manifestations of these few principles are infinitely large. The diversity of physical and biological worlds created by God confuses the observer. Accordingly the problem defining reason is in the sphere of the human perception and cognitive thinking. "Nevertheless mankind is able to recognize in a certain way, even though restricted, the limits of his perspectives and exceed them. He can widen the barriers of his interests and at least partially overcome them" (Pannenberg 1983, 57 et seq.). ["Immerhin ist der Mensch in der Lage, in jeweils bestimmter Weise, wenn auch nur in begrenztem Maße, die Partikularität seiner Perspektiven zu erkennen und so zu überschreiten, die Schranken seiner eigenen Interessen zu erweitern und wenigstens partiell zu überwinden"]. This limited human perspective demonstrates mankind's existence as a created being and the finite nature connected to it.

The possibility of expanding the given barriers and overcoming the tension affects the particular morals of man i.e. this what his conscience dictates to him, and his own passions i.e. interests. Islamic theology understands itself as an orientation within this area of conflict. It shows the dangers, which lead to ruin. It is certain that Islamic theology today in the Western Hemisphere appears as anything but inviting. However, the evidence that Islam is capable of doing something is proved by the seven centuries of the Moors on the Iberian peninsula. This epoch was the only golden age in regards to the relationship of the three Abrahamic religions. Nowadays in the age of the modern achievements one is not able to achieve this. Today humanity is governed more by superficial interests and passions than by God given reason and common sense. A responsible use of reason certainly leads to success in the scientific-technical control of nature. However, by ignoring the Divine corrective, "the achievements of the technical development" – governed by greed - are contrary to entirety of nature. They have a destructive effect.

This line of thinking leads to the realization that according to the whole world and all humanity theology – apart from the particular religion whose function it is - is an essential discipline of the arts.

Mankind owes today's technical development to research in the scientific fields. But the goals which are reached can be abused. Economic interests are the most important which is demonstrated by today's environmental problems. The production of the atomic bomb, which shows a negative use of nuclear energy, is an example that scientific knowledge requires a level of ethics in order to prevent abuse. Therefore it would be wise for physicists to have to deal with ethical problems already in their basic studies – independent of a religious affiliation.

Any education without the basic formation of ethics is simply one-sided and the final aim is not humane. It is extremely doubtful whether this is feasible without the acceptance of a higher all encompassing truth, which enlightens and defines reason. Viewed thusly the mistake of today's modern society is nothing less than a symptom of the lack of faith (cp. Ginaidi 2002).

1.8 Satan as Personification of Human Inadequacy

According to the previous chapters the characteristic didactic of the Islamic Holy Book points out antithetical situations. It occurs this way: God demonstrates by example the way things should be. On the other hand negative things, which should not occur, are clearly revealed. Satan personifies the forbidden things by his behaviour. Here is a clear warning of danger, which signals to humanity from what to refrain. Tilman Nagel sees in Satan, according to Islamic teaching, a creature who was sacrificed through his reason when tempting Adam and Eve to eat from the fruit of the forbidden tree. "So in the decisive moment Satan didn't lose his reason, but was led astray by his contemplation proving to be arrogant toward God. As punishment God drove Satan out of paradise" (Nagel 1994, 30). ["Satan also entschlug sich im entscheidenden Augenblick nicht seines Verstandes, geriet daher mit seinen Überlegungen auf Abwege und erwies sich als hochmütig gegen Gott, der ihn zur Strafe aus dem Paradies vertrieb."] Satan had seduced Adam and Eve to act contrary toward a commandment of God.

This consciously God given attribute, full free will, of course holds many dangers. No one less than God has already made us aware of our own human insufficiencies and our human attributes: "Verily We have created man into toil and struggle." (90, 4) Or "6 He may say (boastfully): "Wealth have I squandered in abundance!7 Thinketh he that none beholdeth him 8 Have We not made for him a pair of eyes? 9

And a tongue, and a pair of lips? 10 And shown him the two highways? 11 But he hath made no haste on the path that is steep. 12 And what will explain to thee the path that is steep? 13 (It is:) freeing the bondman; 14 Or the giving of food in a day of privation 15 To the orphan with claims of relationship, 16 Or to the indigent (down) in the dust. 17 Then will he be of those who believe, and enjoin patience, (constancy, and self-restraint), and enjoin deeds of kindness and compassion. 18 Such are the Companions of the Right Hand." (90, 6-18)

What is called here the "uphill road" is exactly the correct path every human being should take. God has fitted humanity with sense organs in order to distinguish good from evil and this means that reason can automatically be accepted as a means of differentiation.

Any person striving for the good learns in this surah that this is a rocky path. This association implies that each individual has to make an effort to achieve the good. Thus no one can later plead ignorance of what is good. That is the price God demands from humanity as follower. Here God deals with

Adam's children "with His cards on the table". Satan's role is to aggravate the path of good. This means that consciously humanity's path to God is stony and any person who wants to follow it must actually fight with himself.

Therefore Islamic teaching from the Qur'an and Sunnah is nothing other than "guidance" which demonstrates to us the correct use of this God given attribute. Yet is it not enough to obey this only. Furthermore humanity must be able to conquer the famous "weaker self". Specifically in the diaspora a Muslim has greater inner struggles. Here is the more difficult task which demands the whole person. The nature of this struggle includes the individual challenge to remember God's guidance precisely in the correct original form. Muslims living in the diaspora above all else have to understand the motive behind God's revelation, in order to live daily more freely with the witness of the Qur'an.

Obviously humanity has free will, whether they follow the Islamic path of guidance or the path of disobedience prescribed by Satan. God's support which He has given

Adam on life's journey must be handed down to Adam's descendants until the Day of Judgement: "When thy Lord drew forth from the Children of Adam from their loins, their descendants, and made them testify concerning themselves, (saying): "Am I not your Lord (Who cherishes and sustains you)?" They said: "Yea! we do testify!" (this), lest ye should say on the Day of Judgment: "Of this we were never mindful." (7, 172)

This Divine guarantee that Adam's offspring truly accepted His guidance obliges today's Muslims to pass on His words, the Qur'an, to others in the original language received by the Prophet. Without this guidance humanity's God given cognitive ability will be abused. The opposite of this guidance is the personification of Satan who increases negative human passions. These two extremes have to be preserved parallel to each other for posterity. If one of them is missing the tension which demands the greatest jihad in every individual is lost. In this a part of God's wisdom is recognized. In the tension between the guidance of God and the impulse of Satan provoking and intensifying evil proving oneself is demanded. So the contrast is raised up in the wisdom of God.

In order to lighten mankind's heavy burden of temptation, God showed the Prophet Mohammed during the time when he was in Medina how humanity can deal with this problem. This is the precise spirit and purpose of the Islamic Sunnah. During that time the sign's of God's mercy were shown in the way and manner the Prophet exemplified Islam to the Muslims through his own life.

The Prophet's life then should act as a concrete example for every Muslim. Above all the way and manner the Prophet dealt with his fellow men i.e. with his friends and foes, and especially how he understood Islamic teaching, should serve as a paradigm for each Muslim independent from the age and place in which he lives.

How to understand this concretely and apply it today will be demonstrated through examples in the following chapter.

1.9 The Islamic Path to God

The first community in the age of Medina arose at a time of distress. Its background is the will of God. In the battles against the Meccanian superiority God showed the Muslims an example of His mercy and power: "It is not ye who slew them; it was God: when thou threwest (a handful of dust), it was not thy act, but God's: in order that He might test the Believers by a gracious trial from Himself: for God is He Who heareth and knoweth (all things)." (8, 17)

God stood by the small number of Muslims not only in war, but primarily in social interactions in Medina. This time of distress was the bond that held together the individual members of the first community. Here the question must be asked why the highest power in the universe, God, allowed this misery. The greater the individual hardship, the closer he gets to his God created nature. Therefore the original nature of each individual influenced the individual relationships within the community. Only in this way is the larger community in which humanity lives capable of finding harmony with its original nature. From this viewpoint the social structure of Muslims in the age of Medina was actually created by God. This correlation and the question of the social structure in which humanity should live sets aside the human models from further discussions. Whether mankind should live in a communist, socialist or capitalist system is not to be considered. Do today's Islamic societies practise the social form of the first community? This question definitely has to be answered in the "negative" as a result of the current problems with which they currently struggle. The social relationships created by God comprise a treasure of ingenious solutions for the earthly difficulties societies face. To find this treasure one needs to impartiality consider foreign ideas and humbly consider what is not part of one's own frame of reference.

These conditions cannot even exist in Islamic countries, as long as people are chasing the strange phantom of so-called progress and modern spirit.

An example of individual cooperation in the whole of society during the age of Medina and as it should be today is stated in the following verse: "Knowest thou not that to God belongeth the dominion of the heavens and the earth? And besides Him ye have neither patron nor helper." (2, 107)

One has to consider the Almighty in the interaction of people within the framework of society or interaction of individuals toward society as well as society toward the individual. This consideration of the Almighty is the guarantor for an intact social consciousness and the guarantee for successful fighting the own harmful negative passions. This stands against all tendencies, which create explosive tensions in any social context. Exactly this dualism in which humaity exists, represents the eternal fight between good and evil. The Qur'an comprehends a lot of assertions about the Last Day as a reminder to each one to obey God's paths. "Under the imfluence of speculations and visions of the end time Mohammed calls for self-examination, for correct behaviour, so that human beings do not forfeit their salvation. This correct behaviour, the consequence of turning to God, successfully achieves the certainty of salvation created for humanity and is primarily up to the individual" (Nagel 1994, 32). ["Unter dem Eindruck der Ahnungen und Visionen der Endzeit ruft Mohammed zur Einkehr, zum rechten Handeln auf, damit die Menschen nicht ihr Heil verwirken. Dieses rechte Handeln, Folge der Hinwendung zu Gott, des Durchschlagens der dem Menschen anerschaffenen Heilsbestimmtheit, ist zunächst allein Sache des einzelnen."]

The Islamic rites, the five pillars of Islam, are concrete ways for every one to find the way to God. The person who obeys this path not only physically, but also spiritually and mentally, follows the verses in surah 39: "52 Know they not that God enlarges the provision or restricts it, for any He pleases? Verily, in this are Signs for those who believe! 53 Say: "O my Servants who have transgressed against their souls! despair not of the Mercy of God: for God forgives all sins: for He is Oft-Forgiving, Most Merciful." Here God reveals His approach to mankind. He confronts human inadequacy and Satan's effect on humanity with His mercy.

These two verses and similar ones which clearly show God's compassion toward mankind, unfortunately are the source of the notorious Islamic "kismat", that is fatalism. Just the reference in verse 52 of the above quoted surah "Know they no that God enlarges the provision or restricts it, for any He pleases" tempts many a Muslim to assume, that God gives them everything without the necessity of personal contribution. This problem goes so far as to question whether any person is indeed responsible for his manner of behaviour or whether he is remotely controlled by God like a robot. The question of the predestination of humanity basically projects into the previously mentioned dualism. "No misfortune can happen on earth or in your souls but is recorded in a decree before We bring it into existence: that is truly easy for God" (57, 22). This verse is interpreted as a "book of predestination" by some Muslims. The true context of this verse is to show that God knows the past as well as the future and has preordained them, but in spite of this power He has given mankind free will.

The term "al maktub", i.e. "the prescribed", resp. the events for the individual foreordained by God, is always used even today in situations of misfortune. This applies when a person has done his best to avert damage and nevertheless was unsuccessful. Then they say what had happened to them was preordained by God i.e. "maktub". This term indicates a kismat-attitude. The sense of this verse is to comfort a person in just such situations.

"Muslims are afraid of punishment for atrocities, even though each knows about God's mercy and willingness to forgive. Because he is aware that finally everything is in God's hands, he begins each activity in His name – 'bismillah!' –'entrusts the success to Him – 'inscha'allah!' (what God wills, will be) and attributes to God every result – 'mascha'allah!' (what God willed, would be/would happen). In doing so he feels safe in God's providence to whom he comes home" (Hofmann 1993, 85). ["Der Muslim befürchtet Bestrafung für Untaten, wobei er um Gottes Barmherzigkeit und Bereitschaft zum Verzeihen weiß. Weil er sich bewusst ist, dass letztlich alles in Gottes Hand steht, beginnt er jede Tätigkeit in Seinem Namen - ‚bismillah!'-, stellt Ihm den Erfolg anheim - , inscha'allah!' (wenn Gott will) und schreibt Ihm jeden Erfolg zu - ‚mascha'allah!' (was Gott will/wollte). Dabei fühlt er sich in der Vorsehung Gottes, zu dem allemal seine Heimkehr ist, geborgen".]

This quotation truly indicates the correct attitude concerning the activities each individual has to perform in his daily life. "Only if a Muslim has failed despite all efforts in a project or is involved in an accident, is his 'kismat'-attitude useful; he will not despair, not tear his hair out or rend his clothes, but recognize and accept that the events have been 'maktub' (laid down)" (ibid. 85). ["Erst wenn ein Muslim trotz aller Bemühungen an einem Projekt gescheitert oder einem Unglück ausgesetzt ist, kommt seine ‚kismet'-Haltung zum Tragen; er wird nicht verzweifeln, sich nicht die Haare raufen oder die Kleider zerreißen, sondern erkennen und akzeptieren, dass das Geschehene ‚maktub' (festgeschrieben) war."]

Providence constitutes the sixth Islamic article of faith. It inevitably flows out of the worldview from the Qur'an.

"Or that the Unseen is in their hands, and they write it down?" (52, 41) Such verses which include the term "unseen", i.e. also "What! has he knowledge of the Unseen so that he can see?"(53, 35) demonstrate that to be aware of this is one of God's attributes. Now consider the situation of an individual within the framework of his God given freedom. "This eternal conflict will never be settled in order to satisfy logic. For if humans have free will in all their actions, God's omnipotence would suffer. Otherwise: when God preordains – why then is an individual responsible for his deeds?" (Hamidullah 1983, 71) ["Dieser ewige Zwiespalt wird niemals zur Befriedigung der Logik entschieden werden können. Denn wenn der Mensch freie Entscheidung in allen seinen Handlungen hätte, würde die Allmacht Gottes dadurch leiden. Andererseits: wenn Gott vorherbestimmt – warum ist dann der Mensch für seine Taten verantwortlich?"] This quotation describes the problem. When God preordains, why are people held accountable for their deeds? "The Prophet has strongly recommended to his colleagues, not to delve into discussions about this subject…" (ibid. 71). ["Der Prophet hat seinen Genossen sehr eindringlich empfohlen, sich nicht mit Diskussionen über diesen Gegenstand zu beschäftigen…"] This warning is important in this respect because the Prophet has seen a temptation for individuals to rid oneself of personal responsibility. This task is imposed on every human being by God: "39 That man can have nothing but what he strives for; 40 That (the fruit of) his striving will soon come in sight; 41 Then will he be rewarded with a reward complete;" (53, 39-41)

Here God shows exactly what He has imposed on each individual in his freedom during his earthly life. All the other trials are, as mentioned above, nothing other than a human attempt to evade this task. In spite of this Divine order, there have been phases in the Islamic theological history, in which people discuss this without observing the prophetic ban.

The group Dschabrits was formed to emphasize Divine omnipotence. A second group, the Qadarits, developed. They supported the thesis of mens' free will and responsibility. Their representative was Hasan-al-Basri (he died in 728). Both groups referred to the Qur'an. Al-Basri was more a preacher of revival than a theologian. He appealed for repentance and self-discipline. He operated in his hometown Basra, that's why his name is al-Basri. He and his supporters shaped a mystic movement, which exerted a big influence in the Islamic centres of the Omaiyadic empire as Damascus, Kufa and Medina in the seventh century. At that time pious, ascetic members of the community discussed dogmatic, juridical and mystic problems. From these spiritual activities the Murdschiits arose, who entrusted the decision about everything to God, i.e. the condemnation of a sinner should be abandoned to God only. Abu Hanifa (he died in 767), the founder of the Hanafitic Islamic School of Law, more precisely expressed the Murdschiitic attitude thusly: Each believer, as long as he professes Islamic theology and acts on it, will in the end participate in the bliss of paradise, in spite of possible violations of the Divine commandments. Serious sins will be satisfied this way: the sinner stays in hell for a certain time and will be delivered by the Prophet's recommendation to God. It is obvious that this could lead to a little laxer morality. However Hasan al-Basri under no circumstances intended this development (cp. Ende/Steinbach 1991, 58).

Recently the view that humanity has free will despite the omnipotence of God has been generally accepted. But this freedom is within boundaries determined by God. According to Abu Zahra (he died in 1974), a scholar of the Al-Azhar-University, God endows humanity the power to act. With its help an individual is able to translate his ideas into actions. However, the individual cannot step outside God's sovereignty with the consequence of his deeds. Only the will of God determines whether everything that happens either is good or bad, or useful and harmful. Consequently there is no differentiation between preservation and decline, between life and death according to the human benchmark. God decides autonomously absolutely independent from the Creation (cp. Khoury 1987, 857).

Those in the Islamic world don't follow the most current state of this discussion. How the individual sorts the problem out for himself is his own personal concern. For this he has to be answerable solely to God. From my own discussions with some Muslims I noticed that they look upon themselves as instruments of God. As far as that goes there are no problems. But it is extremely incomprehensible and almost scandalous that they leave their livelihood to God according to the motto: God will solve the problem – and this just in the situation of diaspora.

After this ample description of the interaction between God and humanity and how an individual has to deal with himself and God in general, He has as a sign of His mercy revealed Himself to mankind in history. Abraham is one of the first chosen by God. Surah 2, 124 states: "And remember that Ibrahim was tried by his Lord with certain commands, which he fulfilled: he said: "I will make thee an Imam to the Nations." He pleaded: "And also (Imams) from my offspring!" He answered: "But My Promise is not within the reach of evil-doers." This dialogue between God and Abraham is a paradigm for the way how God chooses His Emissaries.

From the Islamic perspective, apart from the Prophets of the Old Testament Moses is valid as the next Messenger. It is stated in surah 2, 51-53: "51 And remember We appointed forty nights for Musa, and in his absence you took the calf (for worship), and ye did grievous wrong. 52 Even then We did forgive you, there was a chance for you to be grateful. 53 And remember We gave Musa the Scripture and the Criterion (between right and wrong), there was a chance for you to be guided aright." The whole history of Israel with the Jewish teaching is manifested in the Qur'an and therewith the Jews as well as the Christians are believers. The following verse 87 in surah 2 clearly shows this: "We gave Musa the Book and followed him up with a succession of Messengers; We gave 'Isa, the son of Maryam, Clear (Signs) and strengthened him with the Holy Spirit. Is it that whenever there comes to you a Messenger with what ye yourselves desire not, ye are puffed up with pride? Some ye called impostors, and others ye slay."

Now to the actual subject of the book, the person "Jesus" from an Islamic perspective. In order to make the connections in the next chapter more comprehensible I have to go into the cultural formation of a name. A name already reveals the origin of his bearer. Generally a person has his first name followed by the first name of his father, grandfather, great-grandfather etc. So everybody is able to realize the sequence of the fathers on the basis of his chain of names.

An example should make this clear: Ali ben Mohammed ben Ibrahim ben Hafez ben ... indicates that Ali is the son of Mohammed and he on the other hand is Ibrahim's son, who is the son of Hafez. These days the term "ben", which means as much as "son of", is generally used more and more rarely. In some cases the last name in the chain of names demonstrates the name of the clan's founder.

Thus the fathers form the chain of names for men as well as for women. If someone wants to insult somebody intentionally he calls him by his first name followed by the first name of his mother. This implies that the father of the called person is unknown, i.e. that he may not have an honourable origin or there have been so many possible progenitors so that the mother didn't know any more from whom he has been begotten.

Against this background of naming customs there is a very famous and very honourable name, which departs from the above-mentioned pattern. This name is Jesus, the son of Mary, "Ibn-Maryam". Islamic theology doesn't note the carpenter Joseph, the husband of Mary. He consciously goes unknown in order to exclude the possibility of human begetting from the beginning.

The author of this book came to know him first in Germany by studying Christian theology. There are Christians who don't believe in the secret of Christ's origin. This phenomenon is unknown in the Islamic world.

2. The Origin of Mary, the Mother of Jesus

In order to explain the origin of Jesus according to Islam, the origin of his mother has to be explored. Jesus according to the statements in the Qur'an was born by the Word of God. In the Qur'an Jesus again and again is named "the son of Mary" in contrast to naming after the father which is usual in the whole Islamic area to this day.

Mary's mother was an aged woman according to the Islamic commentary from Ismael Ben Kuthair (p. 359), who was no longer able to expect a baby. She wished with all her heart to have a child. She promised God that if she conceived she would dedicate the child to God. This example should not primarily be a statement about the circumstances of Mary's birth, but a demonstration of God's power and His dealings with humanity. Surah 3 in the Qur'an is named: Ala Imran (The clan of Imran). Verse 33 of this surah states: "God did choose Adam and Nuh, the family of Ibrahim, and the family of Imran above all people." Further verses of the same surah underline the theological importance of Mary's parents i.e. her origin for the Islamic understanding.

This is not only a historical information for Muslims, but it is in fact an example of God's approach with men He has chosen. Furthermore it is stated in surah 3: "35 Behold! a woman of 'Imran said: "O my Lord! I do dedicate unto Thee what is in my womb for Thy special service: so accept this of me: for Thou hearest and knowest all things." 36 When she was delivered, she said: "O my Lord! behold! I am delivered of a female child!" - and God knew best what she brought forth - "and no wise is the male like the female. I have named her Maryam, and I commend her and her offspring to Thy protection from the Evil One, the Rejected." 37 Right graciously did her Lord accept her: He made her grow in purity and beauty; to the care of Zakariya was she assigned. Every time that he entered (her) chamber to see her, he found her supplied with sustenance. He said: "O Maryam! Whence (comes) this to you?" She said: "From God: for God provides sustenance to whom He pleases, without measure."

Whomever God has chosen belongs to the happy people of the world. According to verse 37 God attended to Imran's wife resp. Mary's mother immediately after the birth of the child. In this critical phase He even took care of food (sustenance) for the mother. This reference in the Qur'an shows Muslims how important Jesus is to God. He takes into account not only the person Jesus but Divine providence begins already with his "grandparents".

Besides it is stated in surah 66, 12: "And Maryam, the daughter of 'Imran, who guarded her chastity; and We breathed into (her body) of Our spirit; and she testified to the truth of the words of her Lord and of his Revelations, and was one of the devout (Servants)." In both verses just quoted Mary is described as the daughter of Imran. The similarity of this name with the Hebrew name "Amram" raises a historical problem here. Therefore, I want to go into in the following chapter.

2.1 The Problem in the Ancestry of Mary

According to the previous quotations Mary, the mother of Jesus, is the daughter of Amram. In a further verse of the Qur'an, surah 19, 28, she is named sister of Aaron. "O sister of Harun! thy father was not a man of evil, nor thy mother a woman unchaste!" In Numbers 26, 59 it is stated: "the name of Amram's wife was Jochebed, a descendant of Levi, who was born to the Levites in Egypt. To Amram she bore Aaron, Moses and their sister Miriam."

The reader may assume that there is a mistake in this reference to Mary (Arabic Maryam) and Miriam of the Old Testament. But there are several centuries between the two personalities. How can this be explained from an Islamic viewpoint?

The Islamic commentary of this verse says: "Aaron, the brother of Moses, was the first in the line of Israeli priesthood. Mary and her cousin Elizabeth (mother of Ayhya) came from the priestly family and therefore they were described as 'sisters of Aaron', or 'daughters of Amram' (Aaron's forefather). Compare surah 3, 35, also. Mary was reminded of her noble parentage and her mother's and father's unprecedented virtuosity. She was reminded how she had fallen, and how much she has dishonoured the names of her ancestors! (Die Bedeutung des Korans 1996, 1383)"

["Aaron, Moses' Bruder, war der erste in der Linie des israelischen Priestertums. Maria und ihre Kusine Elisabeth (die Mutter Ayhyas) stammten aus der priesterlichen Familie und wurden deswegen als ‚Schwestern Aarons' oder ‚Töchter Imrans' (Aarons Vater) bezeichnet. Vergleiche auch Sure 3:35. Maria wurde an ihre edle Abstammung und an die beispiellose Tugendhaftigkeit ihres Vaters und ihrer Mutter erinnert. Wie tief war sie gefallen, sagt man, und wie sehr hat sie die Namen ihrer Vorfahren entehrt!"]

„Ucht" doesn't necessarily mean "sister", but in the female form of „ach" (literally: "brother", "companion") also "female companion". Mary belonged to the line of Levi, respected of its fear of God and virtue.

In the old Semitic usage the name of a person often was associated with the name of a famous ancestor or founder of a tribe. A man from the tribe of Ali accordingly was addressed as "son of Ali" or also as "brother of Ali". Therefore, Mary as descendant from the family of priests and so from Aaron, she was called "sister of Aaron" (cp. ibid.).

According to surah 19, 28 and surah 3, 33 the Islamic commentary arrives at the following conclusions:

a) God has mentioned Adam, Noah, Abraham's and Amram's family especially as examples for fear of God and religiosity whom all mankind should emulate.

b) Mention of their names by the believer is regarded as praise of them.

c) From this it is never permissible to draw conclusions in the ancestral or historical meaning (cp. Ismael Ben Kuthair 1980, 358).

2.2 The Testimony in the Qur'an about the Position of Mary

Here Mary, the mother of Jesus, occupies a unique position. She was chosen by God above the women of all nations to receive the highest gift ever received from God, his Word in human form. Mary's preparations for her future task is obvious from the quotations from the Qur'an mentioned in this chapter.

God reports in the Qur'an how His angels delivered His announcement to Mary. She was chosen among all women to be the mother of Jesus. To this it is stated in the Qur'an in surah 3, 42:

"Behold! the angels said: "O Maryam! God hath chosen thee and purified thee, chosen thee above the women of all nations." This unique revelation of God sent in human form to humanity is so important to God from the Islamic point of view that He already prepared the way through His angels for its reception. The Islamic theology interprets this verse as follows: "The word 'chosen' in this verse is used twice for important reasons. First it refers to Mary's exquisite childhood, for contrary to the established tradition she was chosen for the service in the temple, in an unusual way God provided food and she suffered no physical or moral deficiency. Second, Mary was chosen to give birth to a child without having sexual relations with a man. To this it is also stated in the New Testament in Luke 1:28: 'The angel went to her and said, "Greetings, you who are highly favored! The Lord is with you" (Die Bedeutung des Korans 1996, 157). [„Das Wort ‚auserwählt' wird in diesem Vers aus gutem Grund zweimal verwendet. Es bezieht sich zum einen auf Marias wundersame Kindheit, denn ganz entgegen dem herrschenden Brauch wurde sie zum Dienst im Tempel ausersehen, von Gott auf ungewöhnliche Weise mit Nahrung versorgt und blieb von jeglichen körperlichen oder sittlichen Mängeln verschont. Zum zweiten wurde Maria auserwählt, indem ihr die Geburt eines Kindes zuteil wurde, ohne dass ein Mann ihr beigewohnt hatte. Siehe auch Neues Testament, Lukas 1:28."]

God's expectation of Mary is articulated in verse 43 of the same surah: „O Maryam! worship thy Lord devoutly; prostrate thyself, and bow down (in prayer) with those who bow down." In spite of all advantages God gave to Mary she remains an ordinary mortal. This is stated in the commentary of the Qur'an: "Despite all her miraculous gifts from God Mary is nothing more than a mortal and has no participation in divinity. As all devoted servants of God she is specifically exhorted to pray. At the same time the separate rites of the prayer are specifically directed in order to underline their strict observance. Mary is neither a goddess nor a half-goddess and least of all the mother of God" (Die Bedeutung des Korans 1996, 157). [„Trotz all ihrer herrlichen Gottesgaben ist Maria nichts weiter als eine Sterbliche und hat keinerlei Teilhaberschaft an der Göttlichkeit. Wie alle hingebungsvollen Gottesdiener, wird sie ganz besonders dazu ermahnt zu beten. Dabei werden die einzelnen Riten des Gebets genau angeführt, um damit ihre strikte Einhaltung besonders zu betonen. Maria ist weder eine Göttin noch eine Halbgöttin und schon gar nicht die Mutter Gottes."]

Here it should be mentioned that being chosen by God does not award special rights to the chosen person because before his election this person was destined to be a human being. This is a warning to all imams, clerics and incumbents within an organized religion not to take any personal advantage of their religious position. Quite the reverse, they have the duty in accordance with their vows i.e. their election by the community to set the best example. We are all God's creatures and happy is he who may describe himself as an instrument of God.

It should be emphasized that all of chapter 19 in the Holy Qur'an bears the name of Mary. There she is mentioned in connection with the birth of Jesus. In addition her name is used again and again in the context of naming Jesus. He is usually called "son of Mary" because he doesn't have a human father. This attention to Mary in Islamic theology deals a lot with the common Islamic attitude toward women as mothers in Islam. According to Islamic doctrine the mother is sacred to the child. Generally in the Islamic world they say that the key to paradise is under the feet of the mother.

2.3 The Portrayal of Mary from Islamic Sunnah

In order to complete the picture of Mary from an Islamic viewpoint I have to go into her description within the Islamic Sunnah. A Muslim understands Sunnah by applying the contents of the Qur'an to daily life. During the time in Medina the Prophet Mohammed put the contents of the Qur'an into action, from the year 622 after emigrating from Mecca to Medina. He had intellectual discussions about many verses of the Qur'an with his friends and relatives i.e. his followers by Hadithes (discussions).

"The second key source of Islam is the Sunnah, the exemplary path of the Prophet Mohammed, whose principal task consisted in proclaiming the Divine revelation and interpreting it authentically. The Qur'an describes Mohammed as an archetype and example for the believers" (Lexikon des Islam, 612). ["Die zweite Hauptquelle des Islams ist die Sunna, der vorbildliche Weg des Propheten Muhammad, dessen Hauptaufgabe darin bestand, die göttliche Offenbarung zu verkünden und sie authentisch zu interpretieren. Der Koran bezeichnet Muhammad als Vorbild und Beispiel für die Gläubigen."] A confirmation of this assertion is in surah 33, 21: „Ye have indeed in the Messenger of God a beautiful pattern (of conduct) for any one whose hope is in God and the Final Day, and who engages much in the praise of God." The Prophet's role for the Muslims and the manifestation of the Sunnah is furthermore articulated in surah 7, 157: "Those who follow the Messenger, the unlettered Prophet, whom they find mentioned in their own (Scriptures) - in the Law and the Gospel - for he commands them what is just and forbids them what is evil; he allows them as lawful what is good (and pure) and prohibits them from what is bad (and impure); he releases them from their heavy burdens and from the yokes that are upon them. So it is those who believe in him, honour him, help him, and follow the Light which is sent down with him, it is they who will prosper." Here as a Muslim who masters the Arabic language I have to mention that in the original Qur'an is not written "pagan Prophet" but "ummi", i.e. the Prophet doesn't have a knowledge of reading and writing.

"The manner in which Mohammed lived within his community and carried out his duties as an ideal Muslim, how he led the believers on God's path and established the necessary rules – all this shows clearly his way (Sunnah) and is to be found in the reports and narratives (Hadith) of many various responsible witnesses." (Lexikon des Islam, 612) ["Die Art und Weise, wie Muhammad inmitten seiner Gemeinde lebte und seine Pflichten als vorbildlicher Muslim erfüllte, wie er die Gläubigen auf den Wegen Gottes führte und die erforderlichen Regeln festlegte - all das verdeutlicht seinen Weg (Sunna) und findet sich in den Berichten und Erzählungen (Hadith) verschiedener Gewährsleute."]

The most famous collection of Hadithes is from Buchari. The following Hadith contains references to Mary resp. a comparison with Aischa, one of the Prophet's wives: "3411...Abu Musa, may God be pleased with him, reported that God's Messenger, PBUH(Peace Be Upon Him), said: 'Amongst the men there are many who were perfect; and amongst the women only Asiya, the wife of the Pharaoh, and Maryam (Mary), daughter of Amram, were perfect. But as regards Aischa's excellence, it is like the excellence of a meat dish over and above all other kinds of food" (BU:785). ["3411...Abu Musa, Allahs Wohlgefallen auf ihm, berichtete, daß der Gesandte Allahs, Allahs Segen und Friede auf ihm, sagte: ‚Unter den Männern gibt es viele, die vollkommen waren; und unter den Frauen waren nur Asiya, die Frau des Pharao, und Maryam (Maria), Tochter des 'Imran, vollkommen. Was aber die Vorzüglichkeit von Aischa angeht, so ist diese wie die Vorzüglichkeit eines Fleischgerichts über alle anderen Speisearten."]

In order to understand better these sources the reader should understand, that the first number within the hadith, in this example it is number 3411, means the number of the Hadith in the Sunnah. "BU" in the end of the Hadith means Buchari and number 785 is the number of this Hadith according to his codification. First of all each Hadith always includes the chain of descent, who heard from whom that the Prophet said etc. The next Hadith clearly shows what position Mary has in the Sunnah and therefore her importance for all Muslims in the age after the Prophet. 3431…Abu Hureira, may God be pleased with him, reported that he heard God's Messenger (PBUH) saying as follows: 'Among humanity there is no newborn child who is not touched at his birth by Satan and he begins to cry as a result of Satan's touch. Only Maryam (Mary) and her son (Jesus) are exceptions to this.' To that Abu Hureira mentioned >…and I commend her and her offspring to Thy protection from the accursed Satan.<" (Qur'an 3, 36; BU 787) ["...Abu Hureira, Allahs Wohlgefallen auf ihm, berichtete, daß er den Gesandten Allahs, Allahs Segen und Friede auf ihm, folgendes sagen hörte: ‚Es gibt unter den Menschen keinen Neugeborenen, der nicht bei seiner Geburt von Satan berührt wird, und er auf Grund der Berührung durch Satan zu schreien beginnt. Nur Maryam (Maria) und ihr Sohn (Jesus) sind die Ausnahme davon.' Abu Huraira erwähnte darauf >...und siehe, ich möchte, dass sie und ihre Nachkommen bei Dir Zuflucht nehmen vor dem verfluchten Satan.<"]

The theological significance of Mary for Muslims, whereas she cannot be separated from her son, is shown clearly in the following quotation: "3435...'Ubada, May God be pleased with him, reported that the Prophet (PBUH) said: ‚The one whoever confesses that there is no God but the unique God (Allah), who has no partner, and that Mohammed is His servant and Messenger and that 'Isa (Jesus) is the servant of God and His Messenger and His Word which He has offered to Mary and from His Spirit, and (confesses), that paradise is true and hellfire is true, this person God lets into paradise because of his deeds (on earth)" (BU 788). ["3435...'Ubada,

Allahs Wohlgefallen auf ihm, berichtete, daß der Prophet, Allahs Segen und Friede auf ihm, sagte: ‚Wer bezeugt, dass kein Gott da ist außer Allah, Der keinen Partner hat, und dass Muhammad Sein Diener und Gesandter ist, und dass 'Isa (Jesus) der Diener Allahs und Sein Gesandter und Sein Wort ist, das er Maryam (Maria) entboten hat und von Seinem Geist, und (bezeugt), dass das Paradies wahr ist und das Höllenfeuer wahr ist, den lässt Allah ins Paradies eingehen um dessentwillen, was er (im Diesseits) getan hat."]

These few quotations shall suffice as examples of Mary's importance as recipient of God's Word. The elevation of Mary as a woman in Islamic theology at the beginning of the seventh century when the absolute rule of man in which the male played the role of the sword-bearer and defender of honour and in principle represented everything important, struck the heart of the Arabic manliness like a thunderbolt. Generally women at that time were more or less a "necessary evil". Women were useful for primitive work in tent and to produce children.

The social environment which defined the role of man and woman at this time was like this: People lived together in clans. Every clan consisted of several hundred people and the foundation of life was livestock – mainly camels, goats and sheep. The most important problem was providing pasture for the animals. The pastureland depended on rain. So the people were continually at war with one another in the struggle for pastureland and water for the animals. The people in the clan were either traveling as nomads or they were at war with other clans. The most powerful clan was the clan with the most warriors. For women this meant they had to produce as many sons as possible besides their work for the husband, with the animals and the tent. This reason most of the women asked their husbands to take additional wives was in order to at least have help with the work. When a clan lost a war, their male members were killed or chased away and their female members were taken into the slavery by the victorious clan. This condition defined the social role of men and women.

In this context came the admiration of a woman and above all the mother of Jesus. This had the effect of a spiritual revolution. So the status of women in Islamic doctrine today is absolutely equal to the status of men. Apart from what most of the Muslims in the diaspora situation regard as Islamic, equality of man and woman already began at the first sin. It wasn't Eve who seduced Adam to eat from the Tree of Knowledge, but Satan seduced both of them.

3. Assertions about Jesus from the Qur'an

The person Jesus is of great importance for Islam. Jesus is for Muslims not only a Messenger of God who establishes a religion but in fact he demonstrates a proof of God's power. For these reasons the Qur'an includes a lot of testimonies about this significant personality.

In this chapter I want to proceed as follows:

    1. The Prophecy of Jesus
    2. The Birth of Jesus
    3. Life and Work of Jesus
    4. The "Passing" of Jesus

3.1 The Prophecy of Jesus

In surah 3, 45, where Jesus is announced to Mary by the angels, a historical-Abrahamic confirmation states that Jesus is the Word of God, which God laid into the womb of Mary, i.e. Jesus is definitely according to the latest Abrahamic religion the "Logos" of God.

The most important sentence in this verse is "God giveth Thee glad tidings of a Word from Him:" In this term "Word" is the whole dilemma of the interpretation concerning the misunderstandings between the Oriental and Western exegesis. While the West understands the term "Word" = "Logos" according to the Greek philosophy and so lets Jesus become a "part" of God, the Muslim recognizes this as word nothing other than the pronounced Word of God. So the prophecy to Mary according to this Word is true: It shall be and it will be" (cp. Ismael Ben Kuthair 1980, 363).

In order to get to the bottom of the term "Logos" in the Christian understanding I have to recognize that in accordance with the Old Greek-philosophical way of thinking it is harmonious with the concept in the Qur'an. But John's definition of this term that Jesus is the Son of God must be strongly rejected. The mentality of the people today in the region in which Jesus lived has remained throughout history almost unchanged. Each influential adult is regarded by every needy adolescent as a father without a biological heritage. To this day young people, particularly in rural areas, address elderly people as "father" or "mother" depending on gender regardless of acquaintance. This title spoken by a juvenile invokes a psychological obligation for the adult to intervene in a helpful way. In this manner the adolescent wants to give the adult the impression that he indeed could take part as a parent. This includes not only acceptance of the person as an elder, but primarily shows respect for him. John has taken verbatim the expression for God from Jesus' mouth and used it to define the relationship to God. In the Islamic understanding this would reduce God on the level of created humanity, which neither Christ nor God themselves would have wished.

Generally this is an immense problem in the exegesis of the Holy Books. The exegets endeavour to understand the contents of the Holy Book literally for fear of making mistakes. But they overlook the circumstances i.e. the mentality of the speakers. It will be described later that Jesus sets God's acceptance of mankind in order, therefore he takes the liberty of speaking about God as his father.

R. Paret writes in his commentary of the Qur'an about the term "Word" in this verse following Th. O'Shaughnessy in his work "The Koranic Concept of the Word of God = Biblia et Orientalia 11" Rome 1948, 55, as follows: "Th. O'Shaughnessy primarily views the term 'kalima', as it is applied in the Qur'an to Jesus, as having nothing in common with the Hellenistic-Christian Logos-idea. The way he sees it rather – probably one-sided: that Jesus is called into being through God's creative word: 'Jesus' , then, is rightly called a <word>, that is a creative command or, more explicitly, a <thing decreed> by a creative command." (Paret 1981, 66) [Th. O'Shaughnessy ist allerdings der Ansicht, daß der Ausdruck ‚kalima', soweit er im Koran auf Jesus angewandt wird, nichts mit der hellenistisch-christlichen Logos-Vorstellung gemein hat. Er erklärt ihn vielmehr – wohl zu einseitig – damit, dass Jesus durch das göttliche Schöpferwort in die Existenz gerufen worden ist:..."]

In surah 3, 45 it is stated: "Behold! the angels said: "O Maryam! God giveth Thee glad tidings of a Word from Him: his name will be Al-Masih 'Isa. The son of Maryam, held in honour in this world and the Hereafter and of (the company of) those nearest to God." This is absolutely acceptable for Muslims and they don't have any problems with this. He who creates a galaxy like ours, the milky way, with 200 billions of suns and corresponding planets, such an act of Creation is an easy thing for Him.

In the Islamic literature it is respectively further stated: "This is a prophecy announced to Mary, peace be with her, by the angels. She will give birth to a wonderful boy whose name will be the Messiah Jesus, the son of Mary. He will be very famous among the believers on earth.

The term ‚Messiah' (Arabic wanderer or caretaker) was given to Jesus because he will wander far in order to guide humanity, caretaker because he will compassionately cure people from their illness. All this happens only by means of God's permission" (Ismael Ben Kuthair 1980, 363).

The official Islamic theological belief concerning this verse is interesting: "Word or decision, command. The birth of Jesus was a visible proof of the infinite Divine omnipotence because only by speaking the word 'shall be' was Mary able to conceive without the presence of a male. But these words clearly reject Jesus Christ's divinity. How could he be regarded as God and also accept him as a partner in the divinity of the Creator, after he was created by a command of God? (Die Bedeutung des Korans 1996, 158)" ["Wort oder Entscheid, Befehl. Die Geburt Jesu war ein sichtbarer Beweis der unendlichen göttlichen Allmacht, denn einzig durch das Aussprechen des Wortes ‚Sei' vermochte Maria zu empfangen, ohne dass dazu ein Mann da sein musste. In diesen Worten liegt aber auch die eindeutige Zurückweisung der Göttlichkeit Jesu Christi. Wie konnte man ihn als Gott ansehen und annehmen, er sei Teilhaber an der Göttlichkeit des Schöpfers, nachdem er selbst durch einen Befehl Gottes erschaffen worden ist?"]

In another place speaking to the same verse: Jesus was nothing less than a mortal. He was the son of a completely mortal woman, in no way the son of God. The formulation "son of Mary" points to his humanity and underscores it. One of the wonders of the Qur'an is that this quotation equally refutes the views of Christians and Jews and contains a language that continuously responds to the Christian apotheosis as well as to the Jewish accusations against Jesus.

Mary was expressly created through her relationship to God, piety and fear of God to participate in the miracle. So the angelic message about her imminent conception was received by her the first time. This sign of God includes also a motivation for all people to think about the origin of life. Comparing the genesis of Christ with Adam's genesis was it at Adam's origin a clod of clay or was it more? Only God knows the answer (cp. ibid. 158).

With respect to the relationship between Jesus and God I have had many conversations with Christians friends and theologians over a period of more than 30 years just about this correlation. My following question put the most of them in a difficult position: Regarding to the view "Jesus is the Son of God" why did Jesus say immediately before his arrest in the garden of Gethsemane: "Father, take this cup from me!" Is it to be assumed that Jesus and father, "God", are two different personalities?

The famous argument that Jesus, "God incarnate", consciously emptied his Divine attributes (kenosis) in order to be purely human seems to me a good deal of wishful thinking because the whole earth together with mankind is from today's scientific recognitions less than a dust particle in the universe. Seen from this point of view we have to be more than happy that He has revealed Himself to us anyway.

An important point in the annunciation of Jesus is in surah 3, 46: "He shall speak to the people in childhood and in maturity. And he shall be (of the company) of the righteous." The official view of Islamic theology according to the commentary to this verse is: "The Divine mission of Jesus is said to have lasted only three years, from his 30th to his 33rd year of his life when he was allegedly crucified. But in the New Testament (Luke 2:46: 'After three days they found him in the temple courts, sitting among the teachers, listening to them and asking them questions.') it is stated that Jesus already as a boy discussed with the jurists in the temple and even earlier that 'the child grew and became strong; he was filled with wisdom, and the grace of God was upon him.' (Luke 2:40) In some apocryphal Gospels it is mentioned that he already preached in infancy" (Die Bedeutung des Korans 1996, 158). ["Die göttliche Sendung Jesu soll nur drei Jahre gedauert haben, von seinem 30. bis zu seinem 33. Lebensjahr, als er angeblich gekreuzigt wurde. Doch im Neuen Testament (Lukas 2:46) wird davon gesprochen, dass er bereits als Knabe mit den Rechtsgelehrten im Tempel diskutierte und sogar schon vorher (Lukas 2:40), dass „das Kind aber wuchs und erstarkte in der Fülle der Weisheit". In einigen apokryphen Evangelien ist die Rede davon, dass er bereits im Kindesalter predigte."]

This annunciation of course had a psychological as well as a big educational significance for Mary and her closest family. The psychological importance is from the content of the angels' announcement which prepared her for the education of this "boy wonder". On the other hand the feeling of her own worth is raised so much that she is above common pride.

In my opinion this point is almost a proof for the faith of each individual. I would like to follow up the idea. I maintain that humility is the indication for the individual inclusion in the complete Creation of God. This condition is God's mercy, even as He gave to Jesus resp. his mother. It is not missed by me and my German wife, formerly Roman Catholic, that Jesus shows himself the crown of the Creation. I wonder about the present day competitive spirit raising one's nose over others as a symbol of arrogance and this in a so-called modern Christian society.

The pedagogical element in this announcement is the conscious exclusion of one's own wordly self toward this child (Jesus). This point is very significant pertaining to the interaction between Mary and the child, so that the Divine characteristics with which God endowed Jesus are developing nicely and can be expressed later.

Mary's response to this annunciation was absolutely human, because she knew that a woman needs a man in order to have a child. This is her and our reality in which we live to this day and exactly here we are faced with the problem of modern Christianity in the modern age. She expresses this in surah 3, 47: "She said: "O my Lord! how shall I have a son when no man hath touched me?" He said: "Even so: God createth what He willeth: when He hath decreed a Plan, He but saith to it, 'Be', and it is!" In this place where it is stated: "He said", it means "the angel instructed by God" (cp. ibid.). In this act of Creation an essential element is recognized of His way of causing something to exist. His will is the material from which everything is made. Neither matter nor any other help are required for this.

It is clearly stated in verse 48 of the same surah what God intended for Jesus: "And God will teach him the Book and Wisdom, the Law and the Gospel,". The official view of Islamic theology uses the term "Book" as Scripture. There it is stated: "'Book' could be meant Gospel resp. Torah, also the ability to read and write, capable of reading and writing, that is the revealed Books in general" (ibid. 159).

Jesus' task is the transmission of the Scripture to humanity. According to the current Islamic understanding the term "Holy Scripture" includes the Mosaic as well as the Christian and the Islamic Scripture. The most important subject is that only Jesus is the bearer of God's Message and he himself is not the actual Message. However his origin is a part of God's Message. Also remember, the first word which our Prophet Mohammed heard from the archangel Gabriel, was the command to hear. Refer to the first verses (1-5) of the first surah received. This is surah 96 in the codification of the Qur'an: "1 Proclaim! (or Read!) In the name of thy Lord and Cherisher, Who created, 2 Created man, out of a (mere) clot of congealed blood: 3 Proclaim! and thy Lord is Most Bountiful, 4 He Who taught (the use of) the Pen, 5 Taught man that which he knew not."

Here the imperative "read" is in the original Qur'an in the original language not "proclaim" or "recite" as in other translations. This command was addressed to an illiterate person. In comparison with the command of Jesus, in which the talk is about Scripture, wisdom and teaching, these five verses of the Scripture from the Qur'an make one thing understandably clear: a hidden command is addressed to humanity to acquire knowledge. Our Prophet purposely says in a Hadith: "The ink of a pupil is more sacred than the blood of a martyr." Or: "Acquire knowledge and if it's necessary, even from China!" and China has been a symbol of a distant land for the Arabs on the Arabian peninsula at that time.

In God's revelation the important message isn't about the personality of the Messenger but the content of the Message. For me the use of the greatest gift, which makes us similar to God, the use of mind, is in demand. Especially the natural scientists among believers have an immense religious responsibility, for they have a deeper insight in God's works. It is self-explanatory that each individual has to pursue the path of his own Messenger from God, i.e. the Jew, the Christian and the Muslim are living completely the specific way, which was according his revelation.

In the current process of globalization these followers have use not only of the Abrahamic religions but of the mind which we all have in common. And these followers have to recognize education in the Abrahamic term of Scripture i.e.

wisdom. There is no more beautiful field in which can be observed God's wisdom than the discipline of scientific knowledge.

3.2 The Birth of Jesus

To the birth of Jesus surah 19, 16-35 states:"16 Relate in the Book (the story of) Maryam, when she withdrew from her family to a place in the East." In this verse Mohammed is commanded to mention Mary in his Scripture (Qur'an), for according to God's Laws life in all species of creatures is created by male and female sex. People became so accustomed to this that they forgot the origin of mankind. Now God wanted to give an example of His free power and His will through the birth of Jesus. However this incidence remained unmatched, so that the basic rules are preserved (cp. Die Bedeutung des Korans 1996, 1378).

Islamic theology makes this assumption about Mary withdrawing from her family to a place in the east: "Perhaps in a camber situated in the east, probably in the temple. She withdrew from her family and people in general in order to attend to prayer and worship. It happened in this state of purity that an angel in the form of a man appeared to her. She believed that this was a real man, was afraid and implored him not to disturb her in her seclusion" (ibid. 1379). ["Vielleicht in eine im Osten gelegene Kammer, wahrscheinlich im Tempel. Sie zog sich von ihren Familienangehörigen und den Menschen überhaupt zurück, um sich dem Gebet und dem Gottesdienst zu widmen. In diesem Zustand der Reinheit geschah es, dass ihr ein Engel in Menschengestalt erschien. Sie glaubte, es sei ein wirklicher Mann, fürchtete sich und beschwor ihn, sie nicht in ihrer Abgeschiedenheit zu stören."]

"17 She placed a screen (to screen herself) from them; then We sent to her Our angel, and he appeared before her as a man in all respects." This means the archangel Gabriel. "The interpreters of the Qur'an take the view that he appeared her as a man, so that she listened to him and gained confidence in him and did not reject him, which might have been the case, if he had appeared her as an angel" (ibid. 1379). ["Die Koranausleger sind der Meinung, daß er ihr als Mensch erschien, damit sie auf ihn hörte und Vertrauen zu ihm gewann und ihn nicht abwies, was der Fall gewesen wäre, wenn er ihr als Engel erschienen wäre."]

The term „angel", Arabic „ruh", which is mentioned in this verse, is explained: "The term "ruh" often means "Divine revelation". However, it is occasionally used in order to describe the medium by which such a revelation is announced to the chosen ones by God, in other words, the angel (or angelic-power) of revelation. Since mortal men are not able to perceive angels in their real shape God had him appear in this case as a man in all respects, i.e. in a form which was accessible to her perception. According to Razi the angel is called 'ruh', in order to indicate thereby that these beings are purely spirit, without any physical element" (ibid. 1379). ["Der Begriff ‚ruh' bedeutet oft ‚göttliche Offenbarung'. Gelegentlich wird er jedoch gebraucht, um das Medium zu bezeichnen, durch das solche Offenbarung Gottes Auserwählten mitgeteilt wird, mit anderen Worten, den Engel (oder die Engelskraft) der Offenbarung. Da sterbliche Menschen Engel nicht in ihrer wahren Form wahrnehmen können, ließ Gott ihn in diesem Fall ‚als wohlgestalteten Menschen' erscheinen, d.h. in einer Form, die ihrer

Wahrnehmung zugänglich war. Nach Razi wird der Engel deswegen mit ‚Ruh' bezeichnet, weil damit angedeutet werden soll, dass diese Wesen rein geistig sind, ohne jedes physische Element."]

"18 She said: "I seek refuge from thee to (God) Most Gracious: (come not near) if thou dost fear God." The angel's appearance as man of course frightens Mary.

Surah 19 continues with the dialogue between Mary and the angel who has appeared her as fully human.

"19 He said: "Nay, I am only a Messenger from thy Lord, (to announce) to thee the gift of a holy son." 20 She said: "How shall I have a son, seeing that no man has touched me, and I am not unchaste?"21 He said: "So (it will be): thy Lord saith, 'That is easy for Me: and (We wish) to appoint him as a Sign unto men and a Mercy from Us': it is matter (so) decreed." 22 So she conceived him, and she retired with him to a remote place. 23 And the pains of childbirth drove her to the trunk of a palm tree: she cried (in her anguish) "Ah! would that I had died before this! would that I had been a thing forgotten and out of sight!" During the pains of childbirth she had to keep tight hold of the palm tree. It is extremely difficult for a woman to be left alone during childbirth. To this day the women are accompanied by mostly female relatives during childbirth.

Here her humanity is evident in the most cruel way. Her main problem is how to present this fatherless child to her family. This social dilemma causes her pain anyway and just in this situation a miracle occurs again in the following verse:

"24 But (a voice) cried to her from beneath the (palm-tree): "Grieve not! for thy Lord hath provided a rivulet beneath thee;" It is not definite who has cried to her. In his translation of the Qur'an Rudi Paret thinks that this is the Infant Jesus. The original language states "fanadaha men tahtiha", which means "he cried to her from beneath her." Every simple-minded reader has to assume that this is indeed the Infant

Jesus just leaving her womb. In the commentary of Rudi Paret he writes: "W. Rudolph comments on the circumstances of Jesus' birth (p. 79): 'The most plausible explanation is that Mohammed here is influenced by an event which the so-called pseudo-Matthew has reported in ch. 20 about the escape to Egypt and relates this to the birth: tunc infantulus Jesus laeto vultu in sinu matris suae residens ait ad palmam: flectere, arbor, et de fructibus tuis refice matrem meam...aperi autem ex radicibus tuis venam, quae absconsa est in terra, et fluant ex ea aquae ad satietatem nostram.' The detailed text of Pseudo-Matthew offers (in French translation): D. Sidersky, Les origines des légendes musulmanes dans le Coran, Paris 1933, 142 et seq.) (cp. Paret 1981, 323-324).

This commentary is a slap in the face of each religious Muslim. Furthermore, Jesus was equipped with Divine attributes, which he could use at any time. He used these abilities already as an infant during the escape to Egypt and was already able to display more than ever such a miracle at his birth. It should not be forgotten that this event involving Jesus was God's sign for mankind and that even Islam veryfies this. Therefore, as a Muslim, I cannot understand

Christians who argue belittling the statements in the Qur'an. They forget that at that time scarcely anything had been written down, and what was written existed in today's Israel, while the Prophet and his relatives lived on the Arabian Peninsula. Moreover surah 19 including this verse referring to Jesus was received in Mecca. Furthermore, one must consider that such reports were recorded either in Greek or in Latin and in the age of the Prophet (Mohammed was born in 570) there was according to tradition hardly anyone who was able to understand or read these foreign languages not to mention such documents.

The commentary of the Qur'an says accordingly to this: It was the archangel Gabriel because Jesus spoke for the first time when he was introduced as an infant to Mary's family. If Jesus talked to Mary's relatives as an infant in the cradle, why could he not have spoken to her directly after birth and just in his mother's time of need? Besides, what sense would it make if this was someone else who cried to her from beneath her during the birth? So reason says it was Jesus who cried out. No other being, neither human nor spirit, could console Mary in her situation better than her own son who caused these pains.

"25 And shake towards thyself the trunk of the palm-tree; it will let fall fresh ripe dates upon thee. 26 So eat and drink and cool (thine) eye. And if thou dost see any man, say, 'I have vowed a fast to (God) Most Gracious, and this day will I enter into no talk with any human being'" The commentary of the Qur'an says about verse 26: "Literally: Cool your eyes: an idiom for 'take comfort and be happy'. However, we don't need to lose sight of the literal meaning entirely: she should cool her (perhaps tear-filled) eyes with the water of the brook and take comfort in the fact that she has received an exceptional child. She should also look around and, if somebody approached her, decline any conversation. It was true: she took a vow and therefore she should not speak to anybody" (Die Bedeutung des Korans 1996, 1382). ["Wörtlich: Kühle deine Augen: eine Redewendung für ‚Tröste dich und sei froh'. Wir brauchen die wörtliche Bedeutung jedoch nicht ganz aus den Augen zu verlieren: sie sollte ihre (vielleicht tränenfeuchten) Augen mit dem Wasser des Bächleins kühlen und sich damit trösten, dass sie ein außergewöhnliches Kind bekommen hat. Sie sollte sich auch umsehen und, wenn sich jemand ihr näherte, jedes Gespräch verweigern. Es war wahr: sie stand unter einem Gelübde und konnte deswegen mit niemandem sprechen."]

In another place speaking to the same verse: „In reference to a vow with God she should decline each conversation with other people – men or women. 'Fast' doesn't mean literally abstinence of meals and beverages. She was merely told that she should eat dates and drink from the brook. In this case it means abstinence of common meals and dealings with people generally" (ibid. 1382). ["Mit dem Hinweis auf ein Gelübde Gott gegenüber sollte sie jedes Gespräch mit anderen Menschen – Männern oder Frauen – ablehnen. ‚Fasten' bedeutet hier nicht buchstäblich Enthaltsamkeit von Speise und Trank. Gerade war ihr doch gesagt worden, sie solle Datteln essen und aus dem Bächlein trinken. Es bedeutet in diesem Fall Enthaltsamkeit von gemeinsamen Mahlzeiten und vom Umgang mit Menschen allgemein."]

"27 At length she brought the (babe) to her people, carrying him (in her arms). They said: "O Maryam! truly an amazing thing hast thou brought! 28 "O sister of Harun! thy father was not a man of evil, nor thy mother a woman unchaste!" "Aaron, Moses' brother, was the first in the line of the Israeli priesthood. Mary and her cousin Elizabeth (mother of Ayhya) came from the priestly family and therefore were described by "sisters of Aaron" or "daughters of Imran" (Aaron's father). Mary was reminded of her noble origin and her father's and mother's unprecedented virtuousness. How she has fallen, and how much she has dishonoured the names of her ancestors!" (ibid.1383) [„Aaron, Moses' Bruder, war der erste in der Linie des israelischen Priestertums. Maria und ihre Kusine Elisabeth (die Mutter Ayhyas) stammten aus der priesterlichen Familie und wurden deswegen als „Schwestern Aarons" oder „Töchter Imrans" (Aarons Vater) bezeichnet. Maria wurde an ihre edle Abstammung und an die beispiellose Tugendhaftigkeit ihres Vaters und ihrer Mutter erinnert. Wie tief war sie gefallen, sagte man, und wie sehr hat sie die Namen ihrer Vorfahren entehrt!"]

"29 But she pointed to the babe. They said: "How can we talk to one who is a child in the cradle?" Concerning this the Islamic commentary says: "What could Mary do now? How could she explain the matter? Would they accept her explanation in their critical state? She was only able to point to the infant who, as she knew, was not an ordinary child. And the child helped her. By a miracle he spoke, defended his mother and preached – to an infidel audience" (ibid. 1383). ["Was konnte Maria jetzt tun? Wie konnte sie die Sache erklären? Würden sie in ihrer kritischen Verfassung ihre Erklärung akzeptieren? Sie konnte nur auf das Kind zeigen, das, wie sie wusste, kein gewöhnliches Kind war. Und das Kind kam ihr zu Hilfe. Durch ein Wunder sprach es, verteidigte seine Mutter und predigte – einer ungläubigen Zuhörerschaft."]

"30 He said: "I am indeed a servant of God: He hath given me revelation and made me a prophet;" Here Jesus' significance is clearly demonstrated. He says that he is the servant of God and neither son nor participant in His divinity.

"31 "And He hath made me blessed wheresoever I be, and hath enjoined on me Prayer and Charity as long as I live: 32 "(He) hath made me kind to my mother, and not overbearing or miserable;" Verse 32 explicitly shows how Jesus behaves towards his mother, reverently, contrary to some accounts in the New Testament, see Mt 12:46-50 and Mk 3:31-35.

"33 "So Peace is on me the day I was born, the day that I die, and the day that I shall be raised up to life (again)! 34 Such (was) 'Isa the son of Maryam: (it is) a statement of truth, about which they (vainly) dispute. 35 It is not befitting to (the majesty of) God that He should beget a son. Glory be to Him! when He determines a matter, He only says to it, "Be," and it is."

In reference to verse 35 that Jesus could be the Son of God the commentary of the Qur'an says: "An son is somebody whom transitory beings need in order to propagate themselves or as a help in their weakness. God however is eternal and everlasting. He is powerful and doesn't need help. Everything He creates happens by the word 'Be!' and it is. And what He wants to make real happens according to His will and not by a son or assistant" (Die Bedeutung des Korans 1996, 1385). ["Ein Sohn ist jemand, den vergängliche Wesen brauchen, um sich selbst fortzusetzen, beziehungsweise als Hilfe in ihrer Schwäche. Gott ist jedoch ewig und unvergänglich. Er ist mächtig und bedarf keiner Hilfe. Alles, was Er schafft, geschieht durch das Wort ‚Sei!' und es wird. Und was er verwirklichen will, das geschieht nach Seinem Willen und nicht durch einen Sohn oder Helfer."] In another place the same commentary states: "Begetting of a son is a physical act dependent on the animal nature of man. God is independent of all needs, and it is degrading for Him, to attribute such an act to Him. This idea survives only from pagan and anthropomorphic superstition" (ibid. 1385). ["Die Zeugung eines Sohnes ist eine physische Handlung, die von den Bedürfnissen der tierischen Natur des Menschen abhängig ist. Gott ist von allen Bedürfnissen unabhängig, und es ist entwürdigend für Ihn, Ihm eine solche Handlung zuzuschreiben. Eine solche Vorstellung ist nur ein Überbleibsel heidnischen und anthropomorphen Aberglaubens."] According to the official view of Islam Jesus being the Son of God is neither connected with survival of the species nor with any need of God. As a Muslim living in Germany for more than 40 years and striving for Christian-Islamic dialogue, I understand the Christian view in this way: Jesus is proclaimed as the Son of God in order to express the importance of Jesus to God. The inclusion of God on the level of His creatures i.e. the transfer of human attributes on God hurts God's claim of absoluteness and therefore must be declined.

I intentionally don't want to go into the historical development of Trinitarian teaching at this point. I truly see this problem as a very important demarcation point for Muslims and Christians to approach a mutual understanding of each other intentionally . Only in this manner Christians and Muslims can act according to the Prophet Mohammed and Jesus. Anything else would not be worthy of either personality.

Therefore let's consider the following facts:

In the verses 16-35 Mary is mentioned in the Holy Book because she was chosen by God in order to conceive the Infant Jesus through the Holy Spirit (the archangel Gabriel). This reference to Mary in the Qur'an has three meanings for Islam:

> a) It is a confirmation of the Christian Message, above all concerning the secret of Jesus' origin.

> b) Jesus is the comprehension of God's Word, i.e. here the Christian description of Jesus as God's

Logos is confirmed. Jesus is the proof for God's omnipotence.

c) The way Jesus was brought into being and the teaching he was charged with is as a whole God's sign for all humanity which Mohammed emphasizes in the Qur'an.

3.3 Life and Work of Jesus from the Point of View in the Qur'an

According to the Qur'an the work of Jesus already began in the cradle. Surah 3, 46 states: "He shall speak to the people in childhood and in maturity. And he shall be (of the company) of the righteous." The commentary of the Qur'an accordingly says: "...that the will of God permits the child to speak to people already in the cradle. This miracle shall be God's sign to humanity, so that they recognize the truth that this man was sent by God. And it is the affirmation of the fact that what this child later will speak and do is God's will" (Ismael

Ben Kuthair 1980, 365). This verse was the annunciation of Jesus' birth to his mother Mary through the archangel. As is apparent, a teaching for humanity is already included, and the teaching isn't only through the concrete deeds of Jesus but rather he serves as a tool of God.

The following verses clearly show with which abilities the Almighty Jesus has endowed. The reader should not attribute these miracles recorded not only in the Qur'an but also in the Bible to the ability of Jesus, but rather to God who has endowed Jesus with them.

The miracles of Jesus continue in verse 49 in the same surah: ""And (appoint him) a Messenger to the Children of Israel, (with this message): "I have come to you, with a Sign from your Lord, in that I make for you out of clay, as it were, the figure of a bird, and breathe into it, and it becomes a bird by God's leave: and I heal those born blind, and the lepers, and I quicken the dead, by God's leave; and I declare to you what ye eat, and what ye store in your houses. Surely therein is a Sign for you if ye did believe;"

This verse is understood as follows in an official Islamic commentary: "The miracle of the clay birds is found in some of the apocryphal Gospels; the miracles of healing those born blind and the lepers and raising the dead are found in the canonical Gospels. The original Gospel did not consist in the different narratives which were written later by the disciples, but in the Message pronounced by Jesus himself. It is remarkable in this saying that Jesus spoke with his own tongue as prophesied to Mary by God and that certainly came true at a later time. Jesus makes it clear that each one of 'his miracles' is a miracle of God" (Die Bedeutung des Korans 1996, 159). [„Das Wunder der Lehmvögel ist in einigen der apokryphen Evangelien zu finden; das des Heilens der Blinden und Aussätzigen und des Auferweckens der Toten in den kanonischen Evangelien. Das ursprüngliche Evangelium bestand nicht aus den verschiedenen Geschichten, die erst später von den Jüngern aufgeschrieben worden sind, sondern aus der Botschaft, die Jesus selbst verkündet hat. Das Bemerkenswerte an dieser Ansprache ist, daß sie aus Jesu' eigenem Munde kommt, so wie es Maria von Gott vorausgesagt wurde und später tatsächlich eintraf. Jesus stellt dabei klar, dass ein jedes ‚seiner' Wunder ein Wunder von Gott ist."]

Concerning the Divine miracles which Jesus performed before the people of Israel in verse 49 another commentator of the Qur'an writes correspondingly: "God armed each of His Messengers with abilities appropriate for the age and the people to which he was sent. In the age of Moses magic art was a characteristic of this epoch. This was because magicians were the popular personalities in those days. Therefore God sent Moses and gave him the ability to do magic. That is why the magicians were the first people to recognize God in the works Moses performed. Jesus was sent by God in a period marked by the actions of physicians and natural scientists. God gave him the ability to perform miracles e.g. raising the dead and giving sight to those born blind as a proof of the Divine within his Message" (Ismael Ben Kuthair 1980, 63 et seq.).

A good reference is the time Moses stood in front of the Pharaoh and his magicians. Here God commanded Moses to throw down his staff (Exodus 7: 8-13). The staff became a very big snake, which devoured the snakes of the Pharaoh's magicians. Surah 3, 50 declares: "(I have come to you), to attest the Law which was before me. And to make lawful to you part of what was (before) forbidden to you; I have come to you with a Sign from your Lord. So fear God, and obey me."

Concerning this the Islamic commentary says: "Jesus shows true Christianity: He explicitly confirms the Torah and simply brings some relief from God. For God had forbidden the Jews to do some things, which were previously permitted as punishment for their unfaithfulness. Now Jesus came as a sign of God's mercy rescinding these prohibitions" (Die Bedeutung des Korans 1996, 159). ["Jesus zeigt das wahre Christentum: Er bestätigt ausdrücklich die Thora und bringt lediglich einige Erleichterungen von Gott. Denn Gott hatte den Juden zur Strafe für ihre Untreue einige Dinge, die ihnen zuerst erlaubt gewesen waren, verboten. Jesus kam nun als Zeichen Gottes für Seine Barmherzigkeit mit der Wiederaufhebung dieser Verbote."] Regarding these prohibitions the following example is cited from the New Testament when Jesus relaxed the regulations concerning Sabbath and food. "Then he said to them, "The Sabbath was made for man, not man for the Sabbath. 28 So the Son of Man is Lord even of the Sabbath." (Mark 2: 27-28). God also intended Jesus to be a sign of everyday relief for humanity. The following verses in surah 57 clearly show this: "26 And We sent Nuh and Ibrahim, and established in their line Prophethood and Revelation: and some of them were on right guidance, but many of them became rebellious transgressors. 27 Then, in their wake, We followed them up with (others of)

Our Messengers: We sent after them 'Isa the son of Maryam, and bestowed on him the Gospel; and We ordained in the hearts of those who followed him Compassion and Mercy, but the Monasticism ..."

The official view of the Islamic commentary on verse 27 is: "The main characteristic traits of the Gospel are humility and renunciation of worldly things. The first blessing of God in the Sermon of the Mount is aimed at those who 'are poor in spirit before God', 'mourn' and 'are meek' (compare Matthew 5:3-5). Jesus admonishes his disciples not to worry about tomorrow (Matthew 6:34). Seen with the eyes of a monk these are fragments of an incomplete philosophy. They represent the spirit of Jesus as far as they represent compassion, mercy toward those who suffer and helpful acts. Jesus was extremely compassionate and merciful and influenced his followers to that effect" (Die Bedeutung des Korans 1996, 2647). ["Die hauptsächlichen Wesenszüge des Evangeliums sind Demut und Weltentsagung. Der erste Segen in der Bergpredigt gilt denen, die ‚geistig arm sind vor Gott', denen, die ‚traurig sind', und denen, die ‚demütig sind' (vergleiche Matthäus 5:3-5). Jesus ermahnt seine Jünger, sich nicht um den morgigen Tag zu sorgen (Matthäus 6:34).

Durch die Augen eines Mönchs gesehen sind dies Bruchstücke einer unvollständigen Philosophie. Soweit sie Mitgefühl, Barmherzigkeit mit den Leidenden und hilfsbereites Handeln repräsentieren, repräsentieren sie den Geist Jesu. Jesus war in höchstem Grad mitleidig und barmherzig und beeinflusste seine Anhänger dahingehend."]

Jesus represents the sign of God for "kindness and mercy" toward humanity in accordance with the Islamic understanding. Exactly this Jesus passed on to his disciples according to the New Testament in the Gospel of John, chapter 13: "34 A new command I give you: Love one another. As I have loved you, so you must love one another. 35 By this all men will know that you are my disciples, if you love one another." Furthermore God equipped Jesus with "hikmah" what means "wisdom". Surah 3, 48 and surah 5, 110 attest to this: "3, 48 And God will teach him the Book and Wisdom, the Law and the Gospel". "5, 110 Then will God say: "O 'Isa the son of Maryam! recount My favour to thee and to thy mother. Behold! I strengthened thee with the holy spirit, so that thou didst speak to the people in childhood and in maturity. Behold! I taught thee the Book and Wisdom, the Law and the Gospel ..."

The parallel to this passage is found in the New Testament in Luke 2:46-52, where they have recognized the wisdom of Mary's 12 year old son in the temple: "46 After three days they found him in the temple courts, sitting among the teachers, listening to them and asking them questions. 47 Everyone who heard him was amazed at his understanding and his answers. 48 When his parents saw him, they were astonished. His mother said to him, "Son, why have you treated us like this? Your father and I have been anxiously searching for you." 49"Why were you searching for me?" he asked. "Didn't you know I had to be in my Father's house?" 50 But they did not understand what he was saying to them. 51 Then he went down to Nazareth with them and was obedient to them. But his mother treasured all these things in her heart. 52 And Jesus grew in wisdom and stature, and in favor with God and men." As a Muslim I recognize in these biblical verses how God kept His word to Mary regarding her son's abilities. Here is a kind of compensation from God for her former situation, when she had to appear before her family with an illegitimate child.

135

These previously mentioned sentences refer specifically to the Arabic worldview based on the mentality of that region. Here I want to note that the most of the European theologians forget this point in the interpretation of the Holy Books, whether Mosaic, Christian or Islamic. In this region of the world the former mentality from the age of Christ still exists. A Christian European theologian will view the above-named verses of the Bible only with regard to Jesus and the wisdom bestowed on him by God. No, there is a good deal more behind them as already mentioned concerning his mother and the compensation for her critical situation towards her family.

Let's return again to the statements from the Qur'an in surah 3. Verse 51 states: "It is God Who is my Lord and your Lord; then worship Him. This is a Way that is straight." Here Jesus calls on humanity to serve God and not him. From that it is clear that God and Jesus are two different personalities. For each non-Christian it is completely incomprehensible how it is possible to regard Jesus as God.

Maybe this personification of God in Christ fit a time when earth as a disc represented the whole universe and very little was known about God's Creation. However, today it is known that our own galaxy consists of 200 billions suns and many more galaxies appear in the cosmos as single stars, so this ecclesiastical portrayal of Christ incarnate in its relationship to the individual creates an every widening gap. So it isn't about Christ but in truth it is about God.

Who is God according to Islam? Surah 112 answers this question briefly and incisively: "1 Say: He is God, the One and Only; 2 God, the Eternal, Absolute; 3 He begetteth not, nor is He begotten; 4 And there is none like unto Him." Here the uniqueness of God i.e. His Divine essence is pointed out in a few words. Other attributes of God are described in many other places in the Qur'an. Above all He is the Creator of everything and in no way ascertainable by created man. No matter what work one considers in nature, a certain harmony is always recognizable so to speak as God's fingerprint in His work. One should notice that proper reasoning displays a certain harmony. This means that the individual is in unity with the whole Creation and therefore can recognize this as an indicator for the correct nature of these ideas. That's why it is never proper to consider God's love conveyed by Jesus as love coming from Jesus. Quite the contrary, Jesus was the first allowed to experience this love from God. He deserves respect for conveying God's love. It is not permissible to confuse the Messenger of God with God. Such a disharmony concerning the description of Jesus as "Son of God" i.e. His incarnation, inevitably leads to an inconsistency in faith. A praying person is able to pray to only one God and not to a complexity of three.

Jesus' Message cannot be anything else but theocentric for it basically agrees with the Message of the Torah and all the other Prophets before him. Here it should be mentioned that according to Deuteronomy 13, 1-4, the proof of a Prophet's authenticity is his call for humanity to believe in one God. " 1 If a prophet, or one who foretells by dreams, appears among you and announces to you a miraculous sign or wonder, 2 and if the sign or wonder of which he has spoken takes place, and he says, "Let us follow other gods" (gods you have not known) "and let us worship them," 3 you must not listen to the words of that prophet or dreamer. The LORD your God is testing you to find out whether you love him with all your heart and with all your soul. 4 It is the LORD your God you must follow, and him you must revere. Keep his commands and obey him; serve him and hold fast to him."

The duties of the Christian Message are mentioned in surah 3, 52 et seq., where Jesus himself speaks: "52 When 'Isa found unbelief on their part he said: "Who will be my helpers to (the work of) God?" Said the disciples: "We are God's helpers: we believe in God, and do thou bear witness that we are Muslims." It is evident that each Messenger of God needs his helpers. In this verse is the appearance of Jesus' disciples.

53 "Our Lord! we believe in what Thou hast revealed, and we follow the Messenger; then write us down among those who bear witness." According to the commentary of the Qur'an: "The believer not only swears to believe in God and to follow the path demonstrated by him, but also at the same time to model himself on the Messenger of God in word and deed. This idea always recurs within this surah. – The disciples beseech God for admission among the witnesses of His religion. In support of their statement, they want to become truthful representatives of their belief in order to found a

society based on its principles" (Die Bedeutung des Korans 1996, 160). [„Der Gläubige schwört nicht nur, an Gott zu glauben und den von ihm gezeigten Weg zu gehen, sondern zugleich auch, den Gesandten Gottes in Wort und Tat zum Vorbild zu nehmen. Dieser Gedanke kehrt im Verlaufe dieser Sure immer wieder. – Die Jünger bitten Gott, sie in die Reihen der Bezeuger seiner Religion aufzunehmen. Das heißt, sie in ihrer Aussage zu unterstützen, wahrhafte Vertreter ihres Glaubens zu werden, um nach dessen Prinzipien eine darauf basierende Gesellschaft gründen zu können."]

The concrete works for which Jesus was commissioned are listed in the following verse of surah 5:

a) The confirmation of the Torah before Jesus

b) The revelation of the Gospel

"46 And in their footsteps We sent 'Isa the son of Maryam, confirming the Law that had come before him: We sent him the Gospel: therein was guidance and light, and confirmation of the Law that had come before him: a guidance and an admonition to those who fear God."

This not only includes an acceptance of the Gospel (Arabic Al-Engil), but in point of fact it is a proof of its Abrahamic historical manifestation through Islamic doctrine. Christians are called people of the Gospel (Ahl Al-Engil), as surah 5, 47 demonstrates: "Let the People of the Gospel judge by what God hath revealed therein. If any do fail to judge by (the light of) what God hath revealed, they are (no better than) those who rebel." In this translation indeed "the people of the Gospel", i.e. all Christians are meant and not only Christian scribes. This is also a demand on the owners of this Holy Scripture to conform to its contents. The term "Gospel" in the Qur'an is expressed in two ways, "Al-Engil", as already mentioned, or "Al-Kitab" (the Book).

All places with "Al-Engil" are listed as follows so the reader can visualize the representation in the Qur'an referencing the Gospel.

Verses in Surah 3 about the Gospel

"3 It is He Who sent down to thee (step by step), in truth, the Book, confirming what went before it; and He sent down the Law (of Musa) and the Gospel (of 'Isa)."

" 4 Before this, as a guide to mankind, and He sent down the Criterion (of judgment between right and wrong). Then those who reject Faith in the Signs of God will suffer the severest penalty, and God is Exalted in Might, Lord of Retribution."

"48 And God will teach him the Book and Wisdom, the Law and the Gospel."

"65 Ye People of the Book! why dispute ye about Ibrahim, when the Law and the Gospel were not revealed till after him? Have ye no understanding?" (The People of the Book in this case are the Jewish rabbis and the Christians who disputed about Abraham, whether he is Jew or Christian.)

Verses in Surah 5 about the Gospel

"46 And in their footsteps We sent 'Isa the son of Maryam, confirming the Law that had come before him: We sent him the Gospel: therein was guidance and light, and confirmation of the Law that had come before him: a guidance and an admonition to those who fear God."

"66 If only they had stood fast by the Law, the Gospel, and all the revelation that was sent to them from their Lord, they would have enjoyed happiness from every side. There is from among them a party on the right course: but many of them follow a course that is evil."

"68 Say: O People of the Book! Ye have no ground to stand upon unless ye stand fast by the Law, the Gospel, and all the revelation that has come to you from your Lord. "It is the revelation that cometh to thee from thy Lord, that increaseth in most of them their obstinate rebellion and blasphemy. But sorrow thou not over (these) people without Faith."

"110 Then will God say: "O 'Isa the son of Maryam! recount My favour to thee and to thy mother. Behold! I strengthened thee with the holy spirit, so that thou didst speak to the people in childhood and in maturity. Behold! I taught thee the Book and Wisdom, the Law and the Gospel…"

Verse in Surah 7 about the Gospel

"157 Those who follow the Messenger, the unlettered Prophet, whom they find mentioned in their own (Scriptures) - in the Law and the Gospel - ..."

Verse in Surah 9 about the Gospel

"111 God hath purchased of the Believers their persons and their goods; for theirs (in return) is the Garden (of Paradise): they fight in His Cause, and slay and are slain: a promise binding on Him in Truth, through the Law, the Gospel, and the Qur-an: and who is more faithful to his Convenant than God?..."

Verse in Surah 48 about the Gospel

"29 ...This is their similitude in the Taurat; and their similitude in the Gospel is: like a seed which sends forth its blade, then makes it strong; it then becomes thick, and it stands on its own stem, (filling) the sowers with wonder and delight..."

Verse in Surah 57 about the Gospel

"27 Then, in their wake, We followed them up with (others of) Our Messengers: We sent after them 'Isa the son of Maryam, and bestowed on him the Gospel; and We ordained in the hearts of those who followed him Compassion and Mercy..."

Verse in Surah 19 about the Gospel as Book

"30 He said: "I am indeed a servant of God: He hath given me revelation and made me a prophet;"

The above-mentioned verse speaks of the Book (in the original language) intending the Gospel. It would be absolutely wrong, however, to believe that Jesus received a book in his hands, as some Christian theologians assume. They think that the Prophet Mohammed has taken the Gospel-harmony of Tatian for Jesus' Gospel of the Christians. Both, Jesus and Mohammed, received the Holy Books in the form of inspiration, which they passed on their friends i.e. followers. The term "Al-Qur'an" literally means "this what is to read". It is obvious here that a book is meant. But everybody knows that the individual surahs were received through inspiration by the Prophet Mohammed either in Mecca (Meccanian surahs) or in Medina (Medinian surahs). The book with the codification of the separate surahs however arose in the epoch of the caliph Othman (caliph 644-656) approx. 15 years after the death of the Prophet in the year 632.

In Arabia they spoke about the Qur'an as a book already in the lifetime of the Prophet though it was not yet in its final form. Within the limits of theology we cannot comprehend the truth how the Qur'an was handed down. It is much more profitable to try to understand the social environment and above all the structure of thinking of the age. Unfortunately some occidental reasoning uses analytical thinking, which is very successful in natural science, but leads us astray in theology. Reason is only a part of mental capacity. Reason paired with emotion and intuition together with the attempt to project oneself back to the age of the Prophet is the only wise, conscientious approach. Every theologian no matter which religion he belongs to, is obliged before God and to himself to offer all his mental energies in service to God. A visit to Jerusalem or Bethlehem today will impart to every Christian theologian so much knowledge which he cannot learn at any university apart from the Christian holy cities. It is not without reason that Pilgrimage is the fifth pillar of the Islamic rites required of every Muslim.

God's Message, no matter in which form, is the greatest good God has sent to humanity through His Prophets. A confirmation for this is found in surah, 3, 48: "And God will teach him the Book and Wisdom, the Law and the Gospel." Believers then are required to convey this Divine Scripture conscientiously to their offspring in the clearest form. Precisely here is the problem of the Gospel. Jesus spoke Aramaic. The first written documents about Jesus were authored by Paul, a Jew-Christian, in the Greek language about 50 years later. I don't want to go into the historical problem here of the Bible's origin. One thinks of the apocryphal Gospels etc. As a Muslim it is not my task to discuss these historical discrepancies. But I'm permitted to call attention to these problems in this work. I am motivated to do this by some students in my lectures who took part in the course out of personal interest apart from their subject. Some of them asked me after the lecture how to convert to Islam. This question pains me very much because the Christian Message is as Divine as the Islamic Message as is stated in this book.

As a Muslim living in Germany and engaged in the Christian-Islamic dialogue for more than 30 years, I am afraid of that some Muslims may take the origin of the Gospel as a proof of Christian unbelief. It is claimed that Christians intentionally falsified the Book God gave to Jesus. Therefore, Christians belong to the unbelievers. Many of us don't want to accept that this problem isn't the responsibility of Muslims, but rather a concern between Christians and God. It is certainly also a blasphemy for Muslims when we pronounce judgement on the faith of others.

Summarizing the statements in the Qur'an, Jesus is a Messenger of God who came into existence by God. I have to mention here that there is no doubt for Muslims at all about this. That is because the engagement of Jesus' mother or her marriage to anybody isn't mentioned anywhere in the Qur'an. Joseph is never mentioned in the Qur'an. Jesus' task is the same as Moses' to show humanity the straight path and to proclaim the word of God. However, Jesus' task differs from Moses' task concerning the Divine instruction. The commandments of God for the Mosaic people for example the rules about food are very acceptable for the followers of Moses considering they came out of Egyptian slavery. Jesus did not deliver a symbolical relief from God's commandments, but rather much more. He delivered God's love and above all God's acceptance of all humanity. Furthermore Jesus had the ability to perform many miracles by the will of God. These functioned as an example that he is indeed a Messenger of God.

3.4 The "Passing" of Jesus

Because the Qur'an is a spiritual religious book one cannot expect it to contain concrete comments on Jesus' death. It also does not contain concrete indications where and how Jesus died. Before I specifically go into this chapter, I want to discuss the general subject "the Islamic view of death." In particular I want to do this in consideration of the fact that the language of the Qur'an handles verbs in a very differentiated art and manner. Many verbs are phonetically very similar, but they have absolutely different meanings. I must mention in this connection that the Prophet Mohammed (born 570) came in a time when the socially prominent in society are linguistically more competent than the masses.

During this time the poets were especially the most famous people within society. They embroidered the seven best poems of the year on silk and hung them over the Kaaba. Therefore they spoke of "Al-Muallaqat", which means "the Hanging (Poems)". Their authors were the best and most famous poets until their poems were defeated by others. The Prophet Mohammed had not ever been involved in this activity. All other poetry pales in comparison with the verses of the Qur'an received by him not to mention the theological content to which no other poem had ever referred. This was the proof for some Meccanians that these verses are Divine. This linguistic excursus is necessary to understand this chapter.

From the Islamic view all men must die. The proof for this is found in surah 3, 145: "Nor can a soul die except by God's leave, the term being fixed as by writing. If any do desire a reward in this life, We shall give it to him; and if any do desire a reward in the Hereafter, We shall give it to him..." God's predestination mentioned here is extremely important for a Muslim's whole attitude toward life, because for Islamic understanding death is only a transition from this world to the hereafter.

Surah 21, verse 34 et seq. states: "34 We granted not to any man before thee permanent life (here): if then thou shouldst die, would they live permanently? 35 Every soul shall have a taste of death: and We test you by evil and by good by way of trial. To Us must ye return." From this it is clear that nobody before the Prophet Mohammed ever was immortal.

This would imply that Jesus therefore died before he was recalled to God. In order to differentiate the matter it is necessary to take into account surah 39, verse 42: "It is God that takes the souls (of men) at death; and those that die not (He takes) during their sleep: those on whom He has passed the decree of death, He keeps back (from returning to life), but the rest He sends (to their bodies) for a term appointed. Verily in this are Signs for those who reflect." This verse is supported by Hadith No. 6312 in the Sunnah according to Buchari's classification. "...Huzaifa reported 'The Prophet, peace be upon him, used to say as follows, at bedtime: >In Your name I die and I continue to live.< And when he got up, he said: >All praise is due to God who sent us into life again after He let us die and at Him is resurrection.<" Therefore

sleep is seen similar to death. They also say that death and sleep are cousins or sleep is a lesser form of death."
[„Huzaifa berichtete: "Der Prophet, Gottes Segen und Friede auf ihm, pflegte, wenn er zu Bett gehen wollte, folgendes zu sagen: >In Deinem Namen sterbe ich, und lebe ich weiter.< Und wenn er aufstand, sagte er: >Alles Lob gebührt Gott, Der uns wieder ins Leben schickte, nachdem er uns sterben ließ, und bei Ihm ist die Auferstehung.<"]

Here I offer the following little excursus concerning this prophetic assertion made at the beginning of the 7th century. The actual research about the brain in the field of near death experiences confirms this assertion of the Prophet. The medical assumption that the experience of these persons is nothing more than the final reactions of brain neurons immediately before death has been refuted in America. People who were brain dead reported after regaining consciousness seeing a lighted tunnel. This refutes the above-mentioned assumption that this would be a reaction of neurons in these patients who were pronounced clinically dead.

Thus the first thesis is that Jesus died in his sleep before he was raised by God.

As a Muslim I am very uncomfortable with the heading of this chapter, because Jesus in fact no longer exists on earth, but he still continues to live in heaven, as I will verify later. There is a different view concerning Jesus' crucifixion between Islamic and Christian teaching, because according to the statements in the Qur'an Jesus was not crucified. Surah 3, 55 addresses this problem which was revealed later in Medina: "Behold! God said: "O 'Isa! I will take thee and raise thee to myself and clear thee (of the falsehood) of those who blaspheme; I will make those who follow thee superior to those who reject Faith, to the Day of Resurrection: then shall ye all return unto Me, and I will judge between you of the matters wherein ye dispute."

The term "to take", in German "abberufen", in Arabic "mutawaffika" in this verse is a big problem in the Islamic-Qur'anic interpretation according to the commentary of the Qur'an. The English word "to take" in terms of "to be dead" means "mutawaffa" in Arabic, the infinitive form of this verb is "tawaffa". The following analogous assertions are the result of the question what God means in this connection:

"Qatada and others think that God at first raised Jesus to Himself in heaven and then 'tawaffa'. 'tawaffa' here is understood as Jesus Christ no longer existing for the humans on earth in the conventional form of terrestrial conscience.

Ali Ben Abi Talha Uher Ibn Abbas says that God intends with the phrase 'I will take thee' as Jesus' death.

Mohammed Ibn Ishaq about others according to the chain of tradition thinks that God let Jesus die for the first three hours of the day on which he was raised to God in heaven.

Ishaak Ben Bischr about Idris about Wahab is of the opinion that God let Jesus die for three days, then God sent him back to humanity before He raised him to heaven.

Mater Al Waraq says that the term 'tawaffa' isn't meant in the sense of 'to be dead', but rather 'no more existing on earth'" (Ismael Ben Kuthair 1980, 366).

The most people are rather inclined to use the term "tawaffa" not in terms of "to be dead", but compare it more with the state of sleeping. As confirmation for this interpretation a habit of Mohammed is quoted: After he had slept well he used to say: "Thank God that God wakes us up again after we have died."

The root of this verb is "wfy". As adjective this means "true". Here the question arises what loyalty deals with death. The answer is: Here it means the individual's loyalty to one's own destiny as God determines and defines it. As a human being, I have to remain true to my fate which God imposed on me. The individual should be able to exercise this loyalty voluntarily surrendering to God's will, even joyfully, for death is nothing else but a transition from this world to the hereafter.

It is possible to gather from the diversity of various interpretations regarding God's above-quoted statement "Behold! God said: "O 'Isa! I will take thee and raise thee to myself..." that Jesus was taken to God in such a way that appeared as death to a terrestrial observer. It is important that Jesus continues to live with God. The proof for that is demonstrated in surah 5, 117 et seq. in the conversation between Jesus and God: "117 Never said I to them aught except what Thou didst command me to say, to wit, 'Worship God, my Lord and your Lord'; and I was a witness over them whilst I dwelt amongst them; when thou didst take me up thou wast the Watcher over them, and Thou art a witness to all things. 118 "If Thou dost punish them, they are Thy servants: if Thou dost forgive them, Thou art the Exalted in power, the Wise." In these two verses Jesus accounts for his earthly tasks before God. This means that Jesus continues to live with God in heaven.

Interestingly enough I must mention as a Muslim that the Prophet Mohammed did not enjoy this Divine gift bestowed on Jesus. He died quite normally on June 8th 632 in Medina and was buried there. In these facts are the teachings of the Almighty's absolute sovereignty. It might be assumed that the Prophet Mohammed as the successor of Jesus in the sequence of the religions coming from Abraham should be better off.

I have to guard against putting an own interpretation on this above-mentioned quotation of the Qur'an "Behold! God said: "O 'Isa! I will take thee and raise thee to myself..." because I wouldn't be able to take responsibility for this before God. Only the Almighty knows specifically how Jesus was taken i.e. "mutawaffika."

Finally I want to go into the problem of Jesus' Parousia from the Islamic view. Surah 43, 57 et sqq. refers to it: "57 When ('Isa) the son of Maryam is held up as an example, behold thy people raise a clamour thereat (in ridicule)!" In this verse God speaks to the Prophet Mohammed mentioning the conversation between him and the infidel Arabs.

To that they say correspondingly in the official interpretation of the Qur'an that the pagan Arabs wanted to rank Jesus among the same category as their own idols for they couldn't accept that Jesus was more respected than their idols. They based their claim on the Trinitarian description of God i.e. the ecclesiastical view that Jesus is the Son of God (cp. Die Bedeutung des Korans 1996, 2388). „58 And they say, "Are our gods best, or he?" This they set forth to thee, only by way of disputation: yea, they are a contentious people."

Here God recognized the intention of the infidels and drew the Prophet's attention to their purpose. Concerning this problem the commentary of the Qur'an says: "Their argument was more or less as follows: The Qur'an reveals that Jesus merely was a man – nevertheless the Christians who are called in the Qur'an 'followers of former Scriptures' (Ahl Al-Kitab) regard him as Divine. Don't we then have a right to honour our angels who are surely superior to a human being? – The faultiness of this 'argument' is discovered in the following verse (cp. Die Bedeutung des Korans 1996, 2388) : "59 He was no more than a servant: We granted Our favour to him, and We made him an example to the Children of Israel. 60 And if it were Our Will, We could make angels from amongst you, succeeding each other on the earth. 61 And ('Isa) shall be a Sign (for the coming of) the Hour (of Judgment): therefore have no doubt about the (Hour), but follow ye Me: this is a Straight Way."

This Divine answer to the Arabs (who complained why Jesus should be better than their own deities) defines Jesus exactly as a servant who found special favour with God. The real problem about Jesus' Parousia is in verse 61 where it states: "And ('Isa) shall be a Sign (for the coming of) the Hour (of Judgment)". In Arabic this verse is described as follows: wa innahu la ilmun li-s-sa ati. "innahu" means "that he". In the German translation concerning the problem to whom this pronoun "he" refers, Paret translates it with "Jesus" as well as with "Qur'an". Grammatically this pronoun refers more correctly to Jesus because God just spoke of him. Whether Jesus knows the hour (when the Day of Judgement will come) or he himself is a recognition of it, cannot be determined from the Arabic language of this verse.

The official commentary says: "This is understood as a reference to the second appearance of Jesus in the last days immediately before his resurrection when he destroys false teachings which are disseminated in his name and pioneers for the common acceptance of Islam, the Message of unity and peace, the straight path of the Qur'an.

While the most of the commentators refer the pronoun "hu" to Jesus, some of them connect it with the Qur'an, also, and understand the above-mentioned sentence in terms of 'This (Divine Book) indeed is a way in order to know (that) the last hour (has to come)'. In this connection this shall accentuate the responsibility of every human being in the end before his Creator and also need of our worship due only to Him, therefore this sentence logically follows as a kind of parenthesis to the mention of Jesus' deification" (Die Bedeutung des Korans 1996, 2389). [„Dies wird als Bezugnahme auf das zweite Erscheinen Jesu in den letzten Tagen unmittelbar vor der Auferstehung verstanden, wenn er falsche Lehren vernichtet, die in seinem Namen verbreitet werden, und den Weg für die allgemeine Annahme des Islam bereitet, die Botschaft der Einheit und des Friedens, den geraden Weg des Koran. Während die meisten

Kommentatoren das Pronomen „hu" auf Jesus beziehen, bringen es einige auch mit dem Koran in Verbindung und verstehen den obigen Satz im Sinne von: ‚Diese (göttliche Schrift) ist in der Tat ein Mittel zu wissen, (dass) die letzte Stunde (kommen muß)'. Dies soll in diesem Zusammenhang die letztendliche Verantwortlichkeit des Menschen vor seinem Schöpfer betonen und damit die Tatsache, dass unsere Verehrung nur Ihm allein gebührt, deshalb folgt dieser Satz als eine Art Einschub logisch auf die Erwähnung der Vergötterung Jesu."] It is evident that the Islamic commentators of this verse hold the view that Jesus has to fulfill an eschatological task. Many Christian exegetes as well see in this verse a reference to the comeback of Jesus at the end of time.

In the Shiitic and Sufistic description they talk about the coming of the Mahdi. For the Shiites he is the expected 12th imam who makes sure that Islam gets the upper hand over the globe. The assumption of some Christian theologians that this Mahdi will be the Messiah is not correct.

To the problem of the crucifixion surah 4, 157 et seq. correctly states: "157 That they said (in boast), "We killed Al-Masih 'Isa the son of Maryam, the Messenger of God"; but they killed him not, nor crucified him, but so it was made to appear to them, and those who differ therein are full of doubts, with no (certain) knowledge, but only conjecture to follow, for of a surety they killed him not. 158 Nay, God raised him up unto Himself; and God is Exalted in Power, Wise."

The Islamic commentary correspondingly says to this verse: "God was annoyed about the Jews who maintain here that they have killed Jesus Christ, the Son of Mary, God's Messenger. The irrevocable truth is that they have neither killed nor crucified him. He whom they crucified and killed was someone who resembled him. Afterwards they disputed if the crucified person indeed was Jesus and they all absolutely didn't realize whether in fact it was Jesus Christ. However, the truth is that they claim something whereof they really don't have any idea and they never killed Jesus" (Al Muntachab 1979, 139).

The resemblance of this person who was crucified instead of Jesus (surah 4, 157) has an immense importance i.e. that the Christian who believes in Jesus' death by crucifixion is absolutely in the right. It implies God's will that the Christians precisely believe that.

The second thesis about the death of Jesus must be that God took him alive from the earth (rafa ahu Allah ilaihi) and raised him to Himself. Both theses are held by the interpreters of the Qur'an.

I hope that the Christian reader has recognized the importance of Mary and more than ever the significance of her son Jesus for us Muslims with the examples in the verses quoted so far. These facts are very important for the Christian-Islamic dialogue. Just the process of globalization makes this dialogue not only necessary between the religions with preservation of the respective religious identity, but it is quite necessarily a part of mental pluralism which can enrich both sides.

4. Common Statements about Jesus and Mary in the Qur'an and the Bible as an Elementary Basis for Dialogue between the Religions

In the previous chapters I have discussed the most significant statements about the origin of Jesus and their historical problems (see ch. 2.1 about the origin of Mary). But as Jesus represents the most important person in the Christian teaching and at the same time is a central personality for Islam I want to go into parallel statements in both Holy Books for the following reasons:

1. For the Islamic understanding, Jesus is not only a Messenger of God who has proclaimed His word, but he also he is regarded as a confirmation of God's former Message to Moses. Jesus, however, not only affirms the teaching of Moses but supplements it as well.

2. Just as Moses bears out God's previous Messages, so Mohammed confirms the Christian Message of Jesus and completes it.

As the Jews didn't like to accept the references to Jesus in the Old Testament so probably the Christians also don't like to see the completion of their own teaching by the Prophet Mohammed. Here we have to deal with the historical problem of the religions with Abraham as forefather, i.e. each follower of an Abrahamic religion assumes that the own belief represents the exclusive truth. This would be acceptable, if there were imaginable an approximation of absolute truth. Even natural science shows us that each discovered truth represents time-dependent knowledge. Applying this to all religions it is to recognize that attaining approximately the total truth postulates the concentration of all theological energies for the good. Only then in mutual acceptance and love (behold the path of Jesus as a hint of God!) the greatest possibility could be to achieve absolute truth. Peacefully living together in this world then would be a by-product of such a more intelligent strategy than previously. I am convinced that God benevolently would look at these endeavours, and we are permitted to hope that He also will do His part for us.

In spite of His revelations we have not understood until now to interpret the signs of His love correctly. Unfortunately for everyone of us "the own blessed ego" is a barrier to one's own happiness. As a Muslim I more consciously understand my own Islamic teaching after the 18th year of my life when I came from Egypt to Germany. There I live together with Christians up to the present.

I have comprehended the following verse in the Qur'an (surah 5, 48) only through my life in a Christian country and in numerous conversations with Christian and Jewish theologians: "…If God had so willed, He would have made you a single People, but (His plan is) to test you in what He hath given you;…" As a child in Egypt I always wondered why God doesn't use His omnipotence in order to make only one single people of Jews, Christians and Muslims and of the followers of the non-Abrahamic religions, too. That way He would have spared us a lot. However, during my life in the diaspora situation I recognized that different people represent a part of the Divine wealth because the contrast among them makes it clear to everyone what he can call his own. In other words these Messages (Judaism, Christianity and Islam) represent God's magnificent generosity. I only wonder when we begin to compete among each other in the good in order to pass the test mentioned in the verse above.

To the prophecy of Jesus' birth is stated in the New Testament, Mt 1:18-25:

"18 This is how the birth of Jesus Christ came about: His mother Mary was pledged to be married to Joseph, but before they came together, she was found to be with child through the Holy Spirit. 19 Because Joseph her husband was a righteous man and did not want to expose her to public disgrace, he had in mind to divorce her quietly. 20 But after he had considered this, an angel of the Lord appeared to him in a dream and said, "Joseph son of David, do not be afraid to take Mary home as your wife, because what is conceived in her is from the Holy Spirit. 21 She will give birth to a son, and you are to give him the name Jesus, because he will save his people from their sins." 22 All this took place to fulfill what the Lord had said through the prophet: 23 "The virgin will be with child and will give birth to a son, and they will call him Immanuel"—which means, "God with us." 24 When Joseph woke up, he did what the angel of the Lord had commanded him and took Mary home as his wife. 25 But he had no union with her until she gave birth to a son. And he gave him the name Jesus."

The most important point in this quotation from the Gospel of Matthew is the last sentence of verse 20: "because what is conceived in her is from the Holy Spirit." This prophecy from the angel as it is taken from the text, is confirmed in the Qur'an in surah 3, 45: "Behold! the angels said: "O Maryam! God giveth Thee glad tidings of a Word from Him: his name will be Al-Masih 'Isa. The son of Maryam…".

In my opinion there is no doubt at all in both religions that Jesus is the realization of God's word, as it is concluded from the both statements. I think that this truth represents one of the most important and most elementary signs which God has conveyed to mankind, especially to Jews, Christians and Muslims. The proof of this reality, which at the same time was demonstrated in two Holy Books, at least ought to form one of the main pillars of a bridge for communicating between the Christian and the Islamic religions.

A further reason for a conversation about this two places arises in comparison with the way the two texts are substantiated. If I read the following place in Matthew 1:18 with a critical young Christian: "This is how the birth of Jesus Christ came about: His mother Mary was pledged to be married to Joseph, but before they came together, she was found to be with child through the Holy Spirit", I would assume that Jesus Christ had a physical father, Joseph. If Christians and Muslims have a positive dialogue among themselves then it could be possible to take the text in the Qur'an where nothing is found about an engagement of Mary to Joseph as a further proof that Jesus really is the Word of God delivered to Mary by the Holy Spirit.

I only want to emphasize by this little example that Muslims as well as Christians are able to profit from the historical revelation of the Gospel in the Qur'an. Parallelism of some passages in both Books which chronologically seen have been written over a long period of time intensifies the validity of both and so the Divine truth is supported.

A further problem arises for the critical reader from the fact that in the Gospels of Mark and John Jesus Christ's physical parents, brothers and sisters are mentioned. To this point I want to quote the following from the Gospel of Mark, Mk 6:3 et seq.: "3 Isn't this the carpenter? Isn't this Mary's son and the brother of James, Joseph, Judas and Simon? Aren't his sisters here with us?" And they took offense at him. 4 Jesus said to them, "Only in his hometown, among his relatives and in his own house is a prophet without honor." Here the reader could find a further confirmation for the assumption that Jesus really had a physical father as in some translations of the Bible this verse reads: "He (Jesus) is the son of the carpenter and Mary…" The reader might find confirmation in Jesus' statement: "Only in his hometown, among his relatives and in his own house is a prophet without honor."

It is possible to confront the above-mentioned place in the Bible with the following verse in the Qur'an as a clear corrective action. Surah 19, 21 et seq. states: "21 He said: "So (it will be): thy Lord saith, 'That is easy for Me: and (We wish) to appoint him as a Sign unto men and a Mercy from Us': it is matter (so) decreed." 22 So she conceived him, and she retired with him to a remote place."

Only occasionally it is written in the New Testament that Jesus has been born of a virgin. This fact inevitably allows possible doubt about the virgin birth of Jesus. In my view this doubt is more than ever allowed to arise for a Christian in the 21st century because such a sign from God to mankind never occurred before and most likely will never occur again. Don't forget that here a Muslim pleads the cause for Jesus!

The abilities with which God equipped Jesus are clearly revealed in the Qur'an. Essentially both Books describe the same miracles Jesus performed in his life. As a support of this statement I quote the following verses of the Bible. In Luke 7:12-15 it is written: "12 As he approached the town gate, a dead person was being carried out—the only son of his mother, and she was a widow. And a large crowd from the town was with her. 13 When the Lord saw her, his heart went out to her and he said, "Don't cry." 14 Then he went up and touched the coffin, and those carrying it stood still. He said, "Young man, I say to you, get up!" 15The dead man sat up and began to talk, and Jesus gave him back to his mother."

Besides these miracles a series of further signs can be described, e.g. Lk 7:21 et seq.: "21 At that very time Jesus cured many who had diseases, sicknesses and evil spirits, and gave sight to many who were blind. 22 So he replied to the messengers, "Go back and report to John what you have seen and heard: The blind receive sight, the lame walk, those who have leprosy are cured, the deaf hear, the dead are raised, and the good news is preached to the poor."

I have chosen this quotation from the New Testament above all the others because a great number of miracles performed by Jesus are given here. That these miracles of God only could happen by God's will is confirmed in Hebrews 2:4: "God also testified to it by signs, wonders and various miracles, and gifts of the Holy Spirit distributed according to his will."

A reinforcement for these statements in the New Testament is found in the Holy Book of Muslims in surah 3, 49: "And (appoint him) a Messenger to the Children of Israel, (with this message): "I have come to you, with a Sign from your Lord, in that I make for you out of clay, as it were, the figure of a bird, and breathe into it, and it becomes a bird by God's leave: and I heal those born blind, and the lepers, and I quicken the dead, by God's leave; and I declare to you what ye eat, and what ye store in your houses. Surely therein is a Sign for you if ye did believe;"

A further miracle of Christ which he could do thanks to God's help is verified in surah 5, 112 et sqq.: "112 Behold! the Disciples said: "O 'Isa the son of Maryam! can thy Lord send down to us a Table set (with viands) from heaven?" Said

'Isa: "Fear God, if ye have faith." 113 They said: "We only wish to eat thereof and satisfy our hearts, and to know that thou has indeed told us the truth; and that we ourselves may be witnesses to the miracle." 114 Said 'Isa the son of Maryam: "O God our Lord! send us from heaven a Table set (with viands), that there may be for us - for the first and the last of us - a solemn festival and a Sign from Thee; and provide for our sustenance, for Thou art the best Sustainer (of our needs)." 115 God said: "I will send it down unto you; but if any of you after that resisteth faith, I will punish him with a penalty such as I have not inflicted on any one among all the peoples."

Such points of contact between the Bible an the Qur'an at least invite a meeting at a new level, a level of mutual understanding, living together and not as we have up to the present – I think back to the crusades and about competitiveness concerning the question of who has the better religion – seeking mutual annihilation. Especially today the necessity to get along with each other never is ever so urgent, both teachings make it possible to do this.

177

This situation of the next generation within the Christian as well as in the Islamic world literally calls for a believable religious statement within the both religions. The potential regarding these adolescents is possible if communication with one another happens in the spirit of the both doctrines – and only the pure doctrines.

The incongruent statements in the Qur'an i.e. in the Bible about Mary and Jesus only show the religious limits which must be. Finally, the dialogue should not be a "wishy-washy" dialogue according to the motto: "We all believe in the same anyway." It cannot happen like that!

The following chapter shall present in detail the concrete limits between Islam and Christianity. Precisely here we have an excellent opportunity to point out to one another differing points of view without having the intention to avoid them in any way. We need to have this inter-religious dialogue with the conscious awareness that it is the will of God that there are Jews, Christians and Muslims in their historical order together with their differences. Precisely contrary statements in the Holy Books have the very important function to work for the good with the discussion concerning the matter of God. Only in this manner can each side come to a deeper understanding of one's own doctrine and so Christians and Muslims approach God each on his own path. Exactly this I have experienced with my Islamic tenet in the situation of diaspora in Germany with my Christian German friends.

5. Different Statements about Mary and Jesus in the Holy Scriptures

The greatest discrepancies between the statements in the Qur'an and in the Bible can be articulated in the following five points:

1. The crucifixion of Jesus
2. The ecclesiastical dogma of Trinity
3. The Mariology
4. The teachings about Jesus as Son of God
5. The incarnation of God in Jesus

The most important statements in the Qur'an about the crucifixion of Jesus already have been treated in chapter 3.4, The "Passing" of Jesus.

Now I want to mention the most significant statements in the Qur'an concerning the ecclesiastical dogma of Trinity.

In surah 5, 72 et seq. is stated clearly and unequivocally: "72 They do blaspheme who say: "God is Al-Masih the son of Maryam." But said Al-Masih: "O Children of Israel! Worship God, my Lord and your Lord." Whoever joins other gods with God, God will forbid him the Garden, and the Fire will be his abode. There will for the wrong-doers be no one to help. 73 They do blaspheme who say: God is one of three in a Trinity: for there is no god except One God. If they desist not from their word (of blasphemy), verily a grievous penalty will befall the blasphemers among them."

Here it is clear that Islam clearly refuses the dogma of the Trinity. Indeed I don't know whether a praying religious Christian in fact worships three different deities independent from each other at the same time; I tend towards the view that I don't believe that, for it is contradictory to the natural feeling of the people to distribute equitably a sense of reverence to three godheads. Those called "blasphemous" in the above-mentioned quotation then are the very ones who according to Islamic understanding would worship simultaneously three deities. Concerning this problem there is a lack of very important Christian information for us Muslims. I have learned during my long life in this Christian world thanks to my interest in questions of faith, namely that according to the ecclesiastical doctrine God the Father, Son of God and the Holy Spirit are a Christian manifestation of God.

I consciously speak of needed information, for to tell the truth, this is very hard to grasp. Therefore, I can't speak of a learning process. Presumably I'm not alone with this problem as there are quite a lot of Christians who struggle the same difficulty. The glaring contradictions in the self-conception of both religions could be reduced within the bounds of a dialogue.

Despite all understanding and tolerance towards this Christian portrayal of God as three in one why is it stated then in Mt 4:10, as follows?: "…Worship the Lord your God, and serve him only." Or in Lk 18:19: "Why do you call me good?" Jesus answered. "No one is good—except God alone." This discrepancy between the inference of Christ and the doctrine of Trinity only can turn the Christian believer whose logical ability is already challenged and trained at school, into a schizophrenic person if he wants to maintain his belief. Either that or he unconsciously dissociates from the institutional church in order to protect the faith in the one God.

A further confirmation of God's uniqueness is found in Mk 12:29 et seq.: "29 The most important one," answered Jesus, "is this: 'Hear, O Israel, the Lord our God, the Lord is one. 30 Love the Lord your God with all your heart and with all your soul and with all your mind and with all your strength. There is no commandment greater than these." The Islamic description of God's uniqueness regarding the last quotations of the Bible even clearly is confirmed by the Gospel.

Another example for rejecting the incarnation as well as the dogma of Trinity is taken from a dialogue between God and Jesus in surah 5, 116: "And behold! God will say: "O 'Isa the son of Maryam! didst thou say unto men, 'Worship me and my mother as gods in derogation of God'?" He will say: "Glory to Thee! never could I say what I had no right (to say). Had I said such a thing, Thou wouldst indeed have known it. Thou knowest what is in my heart, though I know not what is in Thine. For Thou knowest in full all that is hidden."

I am very concerned to give an accurate statement of the official commentary within Islam on this verse which follows. However, I beg the reader to differentiate between the author's view and this commentary: "Here it is **not** about a 'misunderstanding of Trinity' as frequently was mistakenly presumed, but about the fact of Christolatry which is an official component of the teachings at all great ecclesiastical denominations and is rejected firmly in different places by the Qur'an and Mariolatry, the adoration of Mary. The latter for example is shown clearly in the following prayer by Catarina of Siena: 'O Mary, Mary you are the temple of Trinity! O Mary you are bearer of fire! Mary you offer mercy! Mary you deliver the fruit! Mary you release humankind, for by suffering of your flesh in Word the world was ransomed. Christ saved it with his suffering and you with pains in body and spirit.' 'Hail Mary' is common knowledge.

It is remarkable that the idealization of Mary comes along with a demonization of the woman till witch-hunt.

The term 'Mother of God' at first was coined by some theologians in Alexandria. Though this term was received very well by the people, the church in the first instance was not declined to accept these teachings and pronounced the adoration of the Virgin Mary as a false belief. At the council of Ephesus 431 AD the term at last was used officially by the church. As a result of that the adoration of the Virgin Mary spread like an avalanche inside as well as outside the church, until in the age of the revelation of the Qur'an the adoration of the 'Mother of God' had overshadowed the adoration of the 'Father' and the 'Holy Spirit'. Statues of her were put up in the churches and she was adored, worshipped, and called on. It was essential to attain her relief and protection as the most important source of Christian confidence. Though the protestants exerted everything after the Reformation in order to fight the adoration of the Virgin Mary, the Catholic Church still hangs on to it" (Die Bedeutung des Korans München 1996, 434). [„Hier handelt es sich **nicht**, wie vielfach fälschlich angenommen wurde, um ein ‚Missverständnis der Dreieinigkeit', sondern um den Tatbestand der Christolatrie, die ein offizieller Bestandteil der Lehre aller Großkirchen ist und im Koran an verschiedenen Stellen entschieden zurückgewiesen wird und der Mariolatrie. Letztere wird beispielsweise in folgendem Gebet von Catarina von Siena verdeutlicht: ‚O Maria, Maria, du Tempel der Dreieinigkeit! O Maria, du Trägerin des Feuers! Maria, du Darbieterin der Barmherzigkeit! Maria, du Gebärerin der Frucht! Maria, du Auslöserin des Menschengeschlechts, denn durch das Leiden deines Fleisches im Wort wurde die Welt losgekauft! Christus kaufte sie frei mit seinem Leiden und du mit dem Schmerz an Leib und Geist!' Das ‚Ave Maria' ist allgemein bekannt. Bemerkenswert ist, dass die Idealisierung Marias einhergeht mit einer Verteufelung der Frau bis hin zur Hexenverfolgung.

Der Begriff ‚Mutter Gottes' wurde zuerst von einigen Theologen in Alexandria geprägt. Obwohl dieser Begriff beim Volk großen Anklang fand, war die Kirche zunächst nicht geneigt, die Lehre zu akzeptieren, und erklärte die Marienverehrung für Irrglauben. Beim Konzil von Ephesus 431 n. Ch. wurde der Begriff schließlich offiziell von der Kirche benutzt. Infolgedessen verbreitete sich die Marienverehrung lawinenartig sowohl innerhalb als auch außerhalb der Kirche, bis zur Zeit der Offenbarung des Koran die Verehrung der ‚Mutter Gottes' die des ‚Vaters' und des ‚Heiligen Geistes' in den Schatten gestellt hatte. Statuen von ihr wurden in den Kirchen aufgestellt, und sie wurde verehrt, angebetet und angerufen. Als größte Quelle christlicher Zuversicht galt es, ihre Hilfe und ihren Schutz zu erlangen. Obwohl die Protestanten nach der Reformation alles daransetzten, die Marienverehrung zu bekämpfen, hängt die katholische Kirche ihr immer noch an."] This quotation shall clearly show the Christian reader that the Islamic world is consciously aware of the history of ecclesiastical development. Even today when many Muslims are accused of abusing their religion in current events wherein they are in the process of finding their identity after century long foreign rule it must be recognized that some people often misuse religion for the love of Christ and others do the same in their desperation for self-preservation. It's high time to examine carefully the interaction between belief, individual and society in order to recognize false motivations, which abuse ideologies. This process requires a certain level of education, which unfortunately proves to be a luxury for the Third World due to the social and economic plight.

The following verse 31 in surah 9 describes the doctrine of Trinity from the view of the Almighty: "They take their priests and their anchorites to be their lords in derogation of

God, and (they take as their Lord) Al-Masih, the son of Maryam; yet they were commanded to worship but One God: there is no god but He. Praise and glory to Him: (far is He) from having the partners they associate (with Him)." This verse in the official commentary of the Qur'an states the following: "The adoration of priests, saints and ascetics is a form of superstition to which people tended in every age. The development of Jewish superstition is obvious from the Talmud; among the Christians it arises from the dogmas about the infallibility of the pope and the adoration of the Saints. The mere thought of a separate priesthood, which is between God and humanity and 'administers sacraments' contradicts the loving-kindness and ever-present grace of God. Polytheism was not limited to the polytheists. Here the deification of Mary's son is mentioned separately, for it still has an influence on a big part of the civilized population (Die Bedeutung des Korans 1996, 773)." [„Die Verehrung von Priestern, Heiligen und Asketen ist eine Form des Aberglaubens, zu der die Menschen in jedem Zeitalter neigten. Die Entwicklung des jüdischen Aberglaubens ist aus dem Talmud ersichtlich; bei den Christen geht sie aus der Entwicklung der Dogmen von der Unfehlbarkeit des Papstes und der Heiligenverehrung hervor. Der bloße Gedanke eines gesonderten Priesterstandes, der zwischen Gott und Mensch steht und ‚die Sakramente verwaltet' widerspricht der Güte und allgegenwärtigen Gnade Gottes. Vielgötterei war nicht auf die Polytheisten beschränkt. Die Vergötterung des Mariensohnes wird hier gesondert erwähnt, denn sie beeinflusst nach wie vor einen großen Teil der zivilisierten Menschheit."] In addition to that permit me to remind the reader of the real function of Christ. He came to humanity as the sign of God's mercy. As an example for that he even relaxed the Jewish regulations concerning food. This sign of mercy is undone by the introduction of the priesthood as an interactive link between the individual and God.

A famous quotation of Cyprian is: Extra ecclesiam nulla salus (No salvation outside church). Here Sundermeier speaks of an undesirable development of the Christian religion, that the church consciously fixes a limit between belief and unbelief and keeps a firm hold on formalities which define people's membership – primarily to church and not to Christianity - by baptism (cp. Sundermeier 1966, 123). It can be clearly assumed from this that a step backwards to the tribal religion occurs here, whereas the church takes on the part of a tribe. "Once again the fundamental separation is established between inside and outside, between foe and friend inherent in the tribal religions, which Jesus conquered" (ibid. 123). ["Die für die Stammesreligionen grundlegende Trennung von

Innen und Außen, von Feind und Freund, die Jesus überwunden hat, wird erneut errichtet."]

„In fact the sense of affiliation to a community gives the feeling of security, but also an amount of fear which is able to degenerate into aggression toward what ever is outside i.e. towards the stranger" (Ginaidi 2002, 28). ["Zwar vermittelt das Empfinden der Zugehörigkeit zu einer Gemeinschaft das Gefühl der Sicherheit, aber auch eine Portion Angst, die in Aggression ausarten kann gegenüber dem, was außerhalb steht bzw. gegenüber dem Fremden."] Cyprian's above-mentioned remark is contrary to the statements of Jesus according to the New Testament in the Gospel of John, ch.14: „2 In my Father's house are many rooms; if it were not so, I would have told you. I am going there to prepare a place for you. 3 And if I go and prepare a place for you, I will come back and take you to be with me that you also may be where I am."

"You" quoted in verse 2 and 3 includes the Jews as well as all people, not only those who have lived in his time but also those who will come in future. Here is the expression of Jesus as a sign of God's love i.e. God's mercy in order to express it in the Islamic understanding.

Now I want to go into one of the most difficult problems between the two religions – Jesus as the Son of God i.e. the relationship of God to Jesus and how this is seen from the Islamic perspective. Here I want to confirm once more that my main concern is to point out everything about Mary and Jesus in the Qur'an in this book, and I hope that the reader is able to use it in a positive manner for himself and in his relationship with God. Surah 5, 17 says: "In blasphemy indeed are those that say that God is Al-Masih the son of Maryam. Say: "Who then hath the least power against God, if His Will were to destroy Al-Masih the son of Maryam, his mother, and all, everyone that is on the earth? For to God belongeth the dominion of the heavens and the earth, and all that is between. He createth what He pleaseth. For God hath power over all things." With these words the view of Islamic teaching is expressed concerning Jesus as the Son of God. The commentary on this verse states the following: "The Roman emperor Constantine who went over from paganism to Christianity chose the latter opinion without more precise knowledge of Christianity. He let his followers fight against their opponents and drove off the supporters of other religious persuasions, particularly those who believed in the exclusive divinity of the Father and the human nature of Jesus.

Jesus brought from his Lord the profession of the one and only God, which all the prophets had delivered. And after his time this monotheistic profession lived on in his disciples and their followers. The Gospel of 'Barnabas', one of the numerous Gospels written in this time, speaks about Jesus as a Messenger of God. Later differences of opinions came out. Some people said: Jesus is a Messenger of God as the rest of the Prophets. Others however said: He is a Messenger in fact but he had a special connection to God. Others again assumed: He is the son of God because he was created without a father; nevertheless he is a creature of God. And later some people asserted that he is God's uncreated son with eternal attributes like the Father. From this latter assertion the teachings of Trinity developed consisting of 'Father', 'Son' and 'Holy Spirit' which is rejected by the Qur'an" (Die Bedeutung des Korans 1996, 359). [„Der römische Kaiser Konstantin, der vom Heidentum zum Christentum übertrat, wählte ohne genauere Kenntnis des

Christentums die letztere Ansicht. Er ließ seine Anhänger gegen ihre Widersacher kämpfen und vertrieb die Anhänger anderer Glaubensrichtungen, insbesondere diejenigen, die an die alleinige Gottheit des Vaters und die menschliche Natur Jesu glaubten.

Jesus brachte von seinem Herrn das Bekenntnis zur Einzigkeit Gottes, das alle Propheten gebracht hatten. Und dieses monotheistische Bekenntnis lebte nach seiner Zeit in seinen Schülern und ihren Anhängern fort. Eines der zahlreichen Evangelien, die damals geschrieben wurden, war das ‚Barnabas'-Evangelium, das von Jesus als einem Gesandten Gottes spricht. Später kam es zu Meinungsverschiedenheiten. Die einen sagten: Jesus ist ein Gesandter Gottes wie die übrigen Gesandten. Andere dagegen sagten: Er ist zwar ein Gesandter, hatte aber eine besondere Verbindung mit Gott. Wieder andere meinten: Er ist Gottes Sohn, weil er ohne Vater geschaffen wurde; er ist aber dennoch ein Geschöpf Gottes. Und schließlich behaupten einige: Er ist Gottes unerschaffener Sohn, mit ewigen Eigenschaften wie der Vater. Aus dieser letzteren Ansicht entwickelte sich die Lehre von der Dreieinigkeit aus ‚Vater', ‚Sohn' und ‚Heiligem Geist', die vom Koran zurückgewiesen wird."] An examination of the historical facts commented on here shows all statements are correct. Indeed Constantine reigned in the time when the Monarchians and the Apologists quarreled. He summoned the Council of Nicäa in 325. There for the first time the teachings of Trinity were expounded as dogma.

The reaction in the Qur'an to the tenet of Trinity is taken from surah 5, 75 et sqq.: "75 Al-Masih, the son of Maryam, was no more than a Messenger; many were the Messengers that passed away before him. His mother was a woman of truth. They had both to eat their (daily) food. See how God doth make His Signs clear to them; yet see in what ways they are deluded away from the truth! 76 Say: "Will ye worship, besides God, something which hath no power either to harm or benefit you? But God, He it is that heareth and knoweth all things." 77 Say: "O People of the Book! exceed not in your religion the bounds (of what is proper), trespassing beyond the truth, nor follow the vain desires of people who went wrong in times gone by, who misled many, and strayed (themselves) from the even Way."

195

For Christianity the belief in Jesus as the Son of God is one of the most elementary pillars of faith. Both religions agree that Jesus is the Word of God given as a sign to humanity. Now it is inevitable to ask the following question: Which relationship exists between a pronounced word and the speaker of this word? From the Hellenistic-philosophical view there is a certain identity of both, the Word and Him who pronounces the Word as just this word means nothing else but the articulation of the speaker's thoughts. Generally expressed, a precise thought gets another form. The intention of this transformation is to determine this thought. It would be possible still to proceed saying: This pronounced thought is a part of the speaker and so Jesus becomes identical to God. Here the question has to be raised whether it is legitimate to superimpose this Hellenistic structure on the thought pattern of Jesus and his disciples who experienced his presence.

According to the following quotations from the Bible which describe and confirm the relationship between God and Jesus I don't have any choice but to accept them, as the Gospel is a Holy Scripture (Al-Engil) sent by God in conformity with the statements in the Qur'an. What the recipients of this Holy

Scripture have made of it historically is a matter between them and God.

The following dialogue between Jesus and the Jews written in the Gospel of John 8:51-59 clearly shows the identity of Jesus to God.

"51 I tell you the truth, if anyone keeps my word, he will never see death." 52At this the Jews exclaimed, "Now we know that you are demon-possessed! Abraham died and so did the prophets, yet you say that if anyone keeps your word, he will never taste death. 53 Are you greater than our father Abraham? He died, and so did the prophets. Who do you think you are?" 54 Jesus replied, "If I glorify myself, my glory means nothing. My Father, whom you claim as your God, is the one who glorifies me. 55 Though you do not know him, I know him. If I said I did not, I would be a liar like you, but I do know him and keep his word. 56 Your father Abraham rejoiced at the thought of seeing my day; he saw it and was glad." 57 "You are not yet fifty years old," the Jews said to him, "and you have seen Abraham!" 58 "I tell you the truth," Jesus answered, "before Abraham was born, I am!" 59At this, they picked up stones to stone him, but Jesus hid himself, slipping away from the temple grounds."

A confirmation about Jesus as the Son of God is to find in the text Luke 1:34 et seq.: "34 "How will this be," Mary asked the angel, "since I am a virgin?" 35 The angel answered, "The Holy Spirit will come upon you, and the power of the Most High will overshadow you. So the holy one to be born will be called[c] the Son of God."

In both above-named quotations the relationship between God and Jesus Christ is described so closely linked that the limits between both are abolished.

Now I want to quote the places in the Qur'an about Jesus as the Son of God. I request the reader not to understand these quotations as a kind of corrective but to notice them as objective informations. The point of my approach is to make an experiment for each one to at first take note of the other's religion. I only can hope that this perception does not lead to a negative reaction but on the contrary it shall constitute a basis for communication.

About the relationship between God and Jesus the Qur'an says in surah 2, 253: "Those Messengers We endowed with gifts, some above others: to one of them God spoke; others He raised to degrees (of honour); to 'Isa, the son of Maryam, We gave Clear (Signs), and strengthened him with the holy spirit. If God had so willed, succeeding generations would not have fought among each other, after Clear (Signs) had come to them but they (chose) to wrangle, some believing and others rejecting. If God had so willed, they would not have fought each other; but God fulfilleth His plan."

Here it is obvious that God has strengthened Jesus with the Holy Spirit. Understandably all miracles performed by Jesus were possible through the aforesaid support from the Holy Spirit. According to Islam the Holy Spirit means the archangel Gabriel. The limits between God and Jesus are clearly defined in spite of this verse. Owing to the absolute importance and uniqueness of its message I want to cite surah 112 once again:

"In the name of God, Most Gracious, Most Merciful. 1 Say: He is God, the One and Only; 2 God, the Eternal, Absolute;3 He begetteth not, nor is He begotten;4 And there is none like unto Him."

It must be taken from this surah that God is not to be identified with the person Jesus. According to Islam God neither was begotten nor did he ever beget and none is like Him.

According to the Islamic conception this equality with God refers to all conceivable fields. To speak here of an identity between God and Jesus or of Jesus as Son of God is a blasphemy according to Islam because by it the Creator is put on a par with His creature. In order to get closer to the Islamic idea or the conception of God the speech from the throne in surah 2, 255 shall be quoted: "God! There is no god but He, the Living, the Self-subsisting, Eternal. No slumber can seize Him nor sleep. His are all things in the heavens and on earth. Who is there can intercede in His presence except as He permitteth? He knoweth what (appeareth to His creatures as) Before or After or Behind them. Nor shall they compass aught of His knowledge except as He willeth. His Throne doth extend over the heavens and the earth, and He feeleth no fatigue in guarding and preserving them for He is the Most High, the Supreme (in glory)." God's knowledge about what appears before and after people's lifespan refers to God's awareness of past events and God's foreknowledge in a person's life.

The following verse in surah 4 is directed to the Christians who want to see in Jesus more than a human being sent by God and strengthened with the Holy Spirit: "172 Al-Masih disdaineth not to serve and worship God, nor do the angels, those nearest (to God): those who disdain His worship and are arrogant, He will gather them all together unto Himself to (answer)."

To sum it up, it can be stated that Islam draws a clear unambiguous line between God and His Messengers ranging from Abraham to Mohammed, including Jesus. The most sacred task of Islamic teaching is to watch over the matter that God's absolute nature is not damaged either by anyone or no thing.

6. Possibilities of a Mutual Understanding as a Basis for Communication

In this chapter we are concerned with two conflicting conceptions, the Islamic and the Christian view. Looking into the contents closer we will find out that it is about the problem of articulating from both positions the point of view of mankind's relationship with God.

The Christian is looking for a relationship with a personified God while in fact the Muslim likewise urgently needs a personal relationship. However, he sees in this interaction God's mercy which can come from the Almighty alone or not, but he may not insist on this from the Omnipotent in His "being" – I hope that I have not committed a sin by my way of articulation – as a person or not. I think that every attempt to personify God provides a temptation for a person in his weakness to try to make the Omnipresent to concrete. That undoubtedly is an unconscious attempt to understand God. If He permitted us to comprehend Him he would be on the level of the thunder-god of whom later was made a slave in the form of electricity.

Therein I see the human attempt to grant human modalities to God, which fail to deal with God's real attributes according to the Islamic understanding. How often humans are confronted with situations, which they psychologically are unable to cope with and suppose that God has done them an injustice? The greatest disadvantage is that this relationship can break up quickly because God has not behaved according to human expectations. Humanization of the Almighty either means a reduction of God to the level of the creature or the engrained desire of the creature rising to God's level. Precisely this had an important effect on me in my situation as a foreigner in Germany. In my home country I learned that Jesus personified precisely the crown of humility. He fought for the weak, poor and leprous. My greeting of a Christian German person on the street in Germany often led him to "shock". He uncomprehendingly looked at me and appeared as if he would examine me. His gaze revealed he was asking: "Why is this stranger saying 'hallo' to me?" He replied to my greeting hastily, mechanically and impersonally as if he just performed an extremely annoying, embarrassing duty. This image of a "modern Christian" was the first shocking experience I had in Germany.

A greeting in the countries of the Third or the Fourth world independent of the Islamic teachings doesn't mean anything else but a personal knocking on my vis-á-vis. He faces this merely human action with decency and politeness for the purpose of meeting the other by displaying a kind expression in order to reply to the greeting. It is not without reason that our Prophet Mohammed one day said that the faith is expressed in the dealings with the fellow men. Just in this sphere of individual religiously conditioned humility is the only level which urgently has to be exercised in this world in order to be allowed to use it later with God.

In the previously raised issue above concerning the religious relationship between God and man I personally recognize one of the most important treasures for humanity in order to talk together in a positive way without touching the most private relationship to God in both religions. Both, Christians as well as Muslims, need a relationship with God. Each one of them needs an experience of God, no matter whether it is positive or negative. It is important that the people recognize an experience with God in their lives. Both parties must be aware of this reality within a dialogue. In addition to this reality there is still another factor, the common negative experience which Christians as well as Muslims have experienced throughout history.

Think of the golden age of the three religions of Abraham from 711 to 1492, the period of the Moors on the Iberian Peninsula, in which the foundations were laid for progress in Europe on many levels of science! After the Muslims' expulsion from Spain a process determing religious identity started. All Islamic and Jewish things were frowned on by the Europeans without consideration for the Islamic achievements at this time for Europe. The age of the inquisition and the burning of witches began. A "Christian" way of life was introduced again with might and force. The consequence was the schism and shortly after the Thirty Years' war, followed by two World Wars from a historic perspective, in which atomic bombs were used for the first time. Without going into the invention of the concentration camps by the Boers in South Africa or the racial discrimination in America I have to wonder today what remains of the belief in Christ.

From the time of the Ottoman rule at the beginning of the 14th century, which was followed by the English and French during the First World War, the Arabic-Islamic countries were without their own identity until about 1950. The legacy of this colonial period led to a political, economic, and educational crisis until today. Today Muslims, therefore, are in a process of finding out their identity, which unfortunately at times has led to religious fanaticism in many areas.

We cannot know whether these historical events are maybe God's will and something positive will come of them nonetheless. We should give it a chance as a test.

According to Islam, God's will is behind everything that happens or does not happen. How can we Christians and Muslims know whether today's disastrous situation on our planet is perhaps a sign from God for all of us to try to work together to overcome the disaster in which we all currently live?

Finally, I want to mention from the Islamic view very important starting points described in the Holy Book, the Qur'an, i.e. the way God's Message to humanity is subdivided into the Jewish, Christian and Islamic prophecy. In addition to the positive statements in the Qur'an about Mary, the mother of Jesus, are others as previously mentioned. A whole chapter (surah 19) in the Qur'an is named after Mary. Furthermore she is the only woman mentioned in the Qur'an by name. Moreover the virgin birth of Jesus and the position of Jesus before God are clearly shown and affirmed in the Qur'an. Here I emphasize once again that the Holy Book of the Christians is a part of the Holy Scripture according to the 3rd article of faith as is confirmed by the following verses in the Qur'an. Surah 5, 110 states: "...Behold! I taught thee the Book and Wisdom, the Law and the Gospel...". Surah 25, 35 says: "Before this, We sent Musa the Book, and appointed his brother Harun with him as Minister;" These both verses define the term of the Holy Scripture for the Muslims. A further confirmation of this statement and above all the expression of equality among all Messengers of God before Him is made clear in surah, 2, 136 as follows: "Say ye: "We believe in God, and the revelation given to us, and to Ibrahim, Isma'il, Ishaq, Ya'qub, and the Tribes, and that given to Musa and 'Isa, and that given to (all) Prophets from their Lord: we make no difference between one and another of them: and we bow to God (in Islam)." Here it would be possible to expect that the Prophet, as the Messenger of God's last Message, would put himself above the other Messengers of God. But this is not stated in this verse. This means that the Prophet has passed on these verses unaltered, which God revealed to him. Here permit me to note that the last verse mentioned above, which explains the equality of God's Messengers, is the foundation of Islamic tolerance to whom we owe the golden age of the three religions of Abraham on the Iberian Peninsula.

I cannot fail to mention one of God's commandments for dialogue among the possessors of the Holy Scripture. Surah 3, 64, states: Say: "O People of the Book! come to common terms as between us and you: that we worship none but God; that we associate no partners with Him; that we erect not, from among ourselves, Lords and patrons other than God." If then they turn back, say ye: "Bear witness that we (at least) are Muslims (bowing to God's Will)."

The sentence "Say: "O People of the Book! come to common terms as between us and you..." is a commandment of God directed not only to the Muslims but precisely to "the people of the Book". This commandment demands Jews, Christians and Muslims to words of reconciliation. God's guidance to conduct a common dialogue cannot be clearer. A further ingredient of the above-named quotation is that we Jews, Christians and Muslims begin within this aforesaid reconciliatory manner to have a conscious regard of each other. Then we can recognize together our mutual problems and take measures in brotherly love against them so that our souls, each on their own path, are allowed to render homage to God.

This dialogue God wills should be in the spirit of talking together and is not to be understood in any negative sense. Here is proclaimed "O People of the Book", and this means that all the three religions are at the same level.

I thank our shared God for the completion of this work!

BIBLIOGRAPHY

Abdullah, Yusuf Ali: The Meaning of the Holy Qur'an, Brentwood U.S.A. 1993.

Abdullah, Muhammad Salim: Islam für das Gespräch mit Christen, Gütersloh 1992.

Abdullah, Muhammad Salim: Was will der Islam in Deutschland? Gütersloh 1993.

Abu Zaid, Nasr Hamid: Ein Leben mit dem Islam, Freiburg 1999.

Al Buhari, Sahih: Nachrichten von Taten und Aussprüchen des Propheten Muhammad, Stuttgart 1991.

Al Ghasali, Abu-Hamid Muhammad: Das Elixier der Glückseligkeit, München 1993.

Al Muntachab: Korankommentar vom Gremium des Korans und der Sunna, Kairo 1979.

BibleGateway.com 1995-2005

Brunner-Traut, Emma (Hg.): Die fünf großen Weltreligionen: [Islam, Judentum, Buddhismus, Hinduismus, Christentum], Freiburg 1999.

Brunner-Traut, Emma: Die Stifter der großen Religionen, Freiburg 1994.

Bucaille, Maurice: Bibel, Koran und Wissenschaft, München 1992.

Bürgel, Johannes Christoph: Allmacht und Mächtigkeit, München 1991.

Die Bedeutung des Korans: Bd. 1-5, München 1996.

Die Bibel: (mit Apykryphen oder die Ganze Heilige Schrift des Alten und Neuen Testaments) nach der Übersetzung Martin Luthers, Deutsche Bibelstiftung Stuttgart 1978.

Ende, Werner/Steinbach, Udo (Hg.): Der Islam in der Gegenwart, München 1991.

Ginaidi, Ahmed: Voraussetzungen für einen interreligiösen Dialog zwischen Christen und Muslimen, Stuttgart 2002.

Grünschloß, Andreas: Der eigene und der fremde Glaube, Tübingen 1999.

Hamidullah, Mohammed: Der Islam, Aachen 1983.

Henning, Max: Der Koran, Übertragung von Max Henning, Stuttgart 1976.

Ibn Rassoul, Abu-r-Rida' Muhammad Ibn Ahmad: Auszüge aus Sahih Al-Buharyy, aus dem Arabischen übertragen und kommentiert, Köln 1989.

Imbach, Josef: Wem gehört Jesus?, München 1989.

Ismael Ben Kuthair: Der Korankommentar, Hg.: Die Al-Azhar-Jugend (in Arabic), Kairo 1980.

Khoury, Adel Theodor (Hg.): Lexikon religiöser Grundbegriffe, Graz 1987.

Kreiser, Klaus/Diem, Werner/Majer, Hans Georg (Hg.): Lexikon der Islamischen Welt, Stuttgart

Kuschel, Karl-Josef: Jesus in der deutschsprachigen Gegenwartsliteratur, München 1987.

Lohse, Bernhard: Epochen der Dogmengeschichte, Stuttgart 1974.

Maudoodi, Sayyid Abu-l-A'la: Weltanschauung und Leben im Islam, Leicester 1978.

Nagel, Tilman: Geschichte der islamischen Theologie, München 1994.

Pannenberg, Wolfhart: Anthropologie in theologischer Perspektive, Göttingen 1983.

Paret, Rudi: Der Koran, Kommentar und Konkordanz, Stuttgart 1981.

Paret, Rudi: Der Koran, Übersetzung von Rudi Paret, Stuttgart 1980.

Schwarzenau, Paul: Der größere Gott, Stuttgart 1977.

Wilckens, Ulrich: Das Neue Testament, übersetzt und kommentiert von Ulrich Wilckens, Zürich 1980.

Edition Noëma
Melchiorstr. 15
D-70439 Stuttgart

info@edition-noema.de
www.edition-noema.de
www.autorenbetreuung.de

www.ingramcontent.com/pod-product-compliance
Lightning Source LLC
Chambersburg PA
CBHW070942230426
43666CB00011B/2536